Ancient Wisdom for
Modern Enlightenment

Jayson Barniske

"If I have seen further than others, it is because I stood on the shoulders of giants"
-Isaac Newton

I dedicate this book to my teachers and to you the reader. Together we perpetuate the tradition of wisdom.

www.JaysonBarniske.com

Copyright © 2017 Jayson Barniske

All rights reserved

ISBN-13: 978-0-692-94071-6

Table of Contents

Introduction 2
Part 1: Utilizing Spiritual Tools 5
Chapter 1: Purpose 6
Chapter 2: Spiritual Energy 24
Chapter 3: Frequencies of the Heart 34
Chapter 4: Living in Harmony 53
Chapter 5: Lighting Your Fire 61
Chapter 6: Spiritual Practice 79
Chapter 7: Developing the Right Attitude 97
Chapter 8: Faith 109
Part 2: Applying the Wisdom of Patanjali 115
Chapter 9: Introducing the Yoga Sutras 117
Chapter 10: Basics Concepts of Yoga Philosophy 125
Chapter 11: The Five Causes of Suffering 146
Chapter 12: The Eight-Limbed Path to Enlightenment 160
Part 3: Modern Enlightenment 191
Chapter 13: Enlightenment for Contemporary Life ... 192
Chapter 14: Krishna and the Bhagavad Gita 197
Chapter 15: Buddha and the Dhammapada 205
Chapter 16: Jesus and the Sermon on the Mount 217
Chapter 17: Illuminating the World 245
Bibliography 255

Introduction

The best way to introduce this work is with the story of my own introduction to the spiritual path. By no means do I claim to be a perfected being. Perhaps the greatest encouragement I can offer the reader is that if someone who has traversed my path can find meaning in spirituality, nearly anyone can. I am reminded of an age-old proverb, "He who comes from the darkest depths of despair sees the light brightest." Within everyone lies enormous potential. My sincerest hope is that this book helps you tap into your inner truth and realize your purpose.

My story begins during my high school years. I grew up as the only child in a privileged family. One way or another, I happened into the great pitfall of drugs. In attempt to save me from hurting myself, acting in great desperation, my parents decided to send me to a boarding school. Unbeknownst to them, this boarding school was not all it advertised to be. While there, I was the victim of physical and mental abuse. Eventually the government of the country in which it was located shut down the school.

I came home on my eighteenth birthday full of rage and the desire for revenge against my parents. In a misguided attempt to hurt them, I decided the best thing to do was to make a failure of my own life. Not long after, I found myself expelled from college and facing serious legal problems. I had to serve three months on house arrest. During this time my anger only grew. I decided the best thing to do was to get into martial arts. All I wanted to do was fight. Physically I fought and argued with those closest to me. Emotionally, I felt I was a failure and fought to keep love from entering my heart. Spiritually, I denied the reality of God in my life.

One night I saw a movie and discovered that the most talented martial artists practiced yoga to hone their skills. I figured I would become stronger, more flexible, and a better fighter if I learned how to do yoga. The next evening, my mother introduced me to the practice of deep breathing. I had an immediate paradigm shift. I tuned into an inner sense of peace previously unknown to me. That moment initiated the beginning of my journey on the spiritual path. I have made many mistakes attempting to travel this higher road. I have also learned my mistakes are my greatest teacher. This book is the culmination of 10 years of in-depth introspection.

At times, I intentionally repeat myself throughout the book. This is to add emphasis to important points. If ideas or philosophies discussed raise doubts or questions in your mind and heart, then I am succeeding in my intention. Take everything with a grain of salt. My goal is to guide you on a journey inward in search of your own true self. I can't really teach you anything. I can merely share with you my experience of my own inner journey. When you begin to ask questions, and seek your own experience of the truth, you have begun your own expedition within.

The teachings of all real spiritual teachers before us represent priceless gems of wisdom. I encourage in depth research of their work as I have undertaken. For this purpose, I include comprehensive suggested readings section at the end of this book.

At various times in your life, you may take different things from this book. Read and reread slowly and consciously. There is never any need to rush as I did not rush in manifesting it. Included are many different meditation techniques. Find what works best for you and disregard the rest. Consistency is the best teacher for any spiritual practice.

The book is divided into three sections. The first section, "Utilizing Spiritual Tools" explains specific prerequisite knowledge that can assist spiritual aspirants of any level to deepen their experience. The section discusses purpose, spiritual energy, transforming obstacles into opportunity, staying inspired, maintaining a spiritual practice, and many other topics. This section includes several different meditation techniques previously alluded to.

The second section of this book is "Accessing the Wisdom of Patanjali and the Yogic Philosophy". Patanjali was a revolutionary Indian sage who created a scientific method in the form of an eight-limbed path to attain enlightenment. I discuss his method in depth and many other pertinent ideologies of the basic philosophies in the yogic system.

The third section is the dessert of this work, "Modern Enlightenment." I describe what an enlightened individual looks like in today's world. How would they traverse through the struggles in our society? How do they carry themselves in relationships and service for mankind? In this section, I devote a large portion of material to explaining one chapter from each of the following teachings: Krishna in the Bhagavad Gita, Buddha in the Dhammapada, and Jesus's sermon on the mount in the book of Matthew. This portion of the book discusses the practical application of these master's teachings in our modern lives and how we can attain the levels of consciousness they knew.

It is with a sense of great humility and immense gratitude I offer these teachings to you. If they have one-tenth of the impact in your life as they have had on mine, you will experience unprecedented transformation and the world will be all the much better for it. I honor you for embarking on this journey to the depths of your soul.

Namaste,

Jayson Barniske

Part 1:

Utilizing Spiritual Tools

Chapter 1: Purpose

"Being spiritual has nothing to do with what you believe and everything to do with your state of consciousness"

-Eckhart Tolle

Every spiritual revolutionary has a clear vision of his or her life's purpose and is an active participant in creating that destiny thereby transforming the world. What exactly is a purpose? What are the inner and outer, the minor and major, and the individual and collective purpose? How do I find and start connecting to my own unique individual life's purpose? All these questions are more will be answered throughout the course of this chapter.

The best way to realize one's immediate purpose is to connect to and be conscious in the present moment. Being conscious in the here and now allows an individual to confront the current task at hand. The divine will be always in play. The best way to live in accordance with that will is to live in awareness and with mindfulness of what is happening in each moment.

Ignoring what is happening in the moment because of a preoccupation with the past or future prevents us from realizing our purpose in the present moment. By focusing on the past, we invite regret or sadness into life by indulging in memories of events that are long gone. By entertaining thoughts of the future, we invite worry or fear in our lives by again delving into things that are out of our control and essentially out of existence.

The present moment is the only one that exists. Past and future only exist in thought. Our memories of past events and thoughts of future events do not exist in the physical world.

Rather the past and future only exist in the realm of the mind. Maintaining a focus on the present moment eradicates sadness and fear because in a state of presence the current moment unfolds in front of your eyes without judgment. Dealing with the current situation that presents itself in the here and now is the most immediate purpose in life.

The overall task of constructing a skyscraper could never be actualized unless the contractor screws on the bolt that is in front of him at the current moment. By focusing on installing one single bolt at a time, the daunting and overwhelming fear of the enormity of the project vanishes. In the here and now, things become much more clear and simple. Purpose becomes direct and achievable. The only way to complete a marathon is to take one individual step at a time. The first step is followed by another. Strung together, thousands of steps comprise the twenty-six-mile journey. But you can only take one step at a time. So why focus on anything but the current step?

Inner and Outer Purpose

Everyone has both an inner and outer purpose. The inner purpose is collective. The outer purpose is entirely unique. The inner purpose is to find or connect with God. The outer purpose is manifesting God in the world around us. The highest goal of all existence is to realize the divine. We are not human beings having a spiritual experience rather we are spiritual beings having a human experience. Recognizing this truth within is the inner purpose of life. It is the main reason you and every single human being on the planet has manifested into his or her current form. This is the main purpose your soul has chosen to take physical form. The soul came from a place of ultimate unity with the divine. When the soul incarnates into the body, illusion diffuses into the individual psyche and obscures the truth.

Knowing you are not just the body and identifying with the divine are two very separate states of existence. I can say, "I know I am not my body" and understand the theory without living that reality consciously. Living in awareness of this ultimate truth allows an individual to transcend all suffering and merge with the divine will. Recognizing the Big Self is the highest purpose of life.

Seeking the inner purpose leads the individual and the collective forward in the process of physical, mental, and spiritual evolution. Mankind has reached a plateau in its development. As a species, we have mastered our physical environment. The need for further physical evolution is not currently present. With the advent of so much technology our society has demonstrated many signs of physical devolution. Focusing on computer screens from early childhood, our youth are already experiencing decreased visual ability and showing signs of overly internally rotated posture resembling that of primates.

Turning away from the stimulus of modern civilization and cultivating internal versus external sensory awareness is the best way to realign one's self with inner purpose. Yoga, Tai Chi, Meditation, prayer and many other forms of ancient spiritual practices are effective methods to direct attention inward. Instead of turning the music up to tune out on the way home from work, drive home in silence to tune back into reality. Refocusing energy inward is the way to realign the little self with the Big Self and reconnect to the inner purpose. The inner purpose must be the main priority before any outer purpose can develop. Maintaining a consistent daily spiritual practice through the good times and the bad keeps the spiritual revolutionary grounded and able to manifest his or her outer purpose.

If the inner purpose is connecting to God, the outer purpose is making God a reality. The outer purpose is making the divine reality an actuality in the physical world not only for the self but also for others. The outer purpose correlates with the process of realizing individual destiny. Consciousness of each moment, living in accordance with a specific system of values in alignment with the inner purpose guides the individual on the path of outer purpose.

The highest aspiration of the Self is to serve others. In meditation, probe your mind for what cause most attracts you. Ask yourself, "What am I most passionate about in my life"? Once you realize your calling, analyze whether your current work role is in alignment with this calling. For me, I had a poignant realization one night during a meditation that serving others was the path to enlightenment. Time is the most precious un- renewable resource in life. Teaching yoga and being a spiritual guide is my outer purpose.

During an economic recession, I was working as a real estate agent. Short sales were popular at that time. This was when banks encouraged people to leave their homes to save their credit. I completed many of these types of transactions. I personally benefited by helping banks evict families from their homes. I internalized the karmic consequence for my actions during meditation. In an act of rigorous self-honesty, I admitted to myself that working in real estate was not in alignment with my values. I am not saying that being a realtor is bad. Helping people acquire homes is a wonderful and important task and may be the purpose in life for some. For me, the career path was misaligned with my outer purpose. I decided to leave real estate and open a yoga studio. I must mention before I left, I helped a favorite Junior High teacher sell her rental home and save her credit. This too was also part of my purpose.

Connecting to one's outer purpose is an entirely personal experience. Every individual has his or her own unique outer purpose. This outer purpose is manifesting God's specific plan, or will, for your life. No two people have the same outer purpose. Living it begins in the present moment. Focusing on the here and now is the first most critical step in the process.

Dealing with each task at hand in the present moment is living with a heightened sense of mindfulness toward purpose. Getting lost in thought of past or future occurrences leads to a point of stalemate, a dormancy in living on purpose.

When a person has connected to their inner purpose and found God within, that person accepts the purpose in all things. Every situation in life is guiding the individual on a higher path aimed at accomplishing a specific means of service for others. Realizing God's plan for me required me to accept the things I did not understand. The process of orienting myself toward God's will was not always comfortable or enjoyable, but accepting each situation allowed me to continue moving forward toward my predestined target.

It begins the moment we are born. We are constantly being guided on the path to realize outer purpose. To avoid writing a book on my unique personal story, I will explain a portion of my story of guidance toward outer purpose beginning in my youth. This is a very short version of a much longer story.

I started using drugs in high school and quickly lost all focus in working toward my future. I stopped participating in sports and eventually stopped going to school altogether. Looking back, the process seems to have happened in very rapid succession. My parents were at a loss for words and had no idea how to help me refocus. It was suggested to them that I be sent to a long-term drug treatment program. One night at four in the morning while asleep on the couch experiencing my weekly come down from drugs, I was awoken by two large escorts tasked with taking me to this program. I fell back to sleep. The next time I awoke, I saw the sign for the Mexico/US border crossing.

My parents chose to send me to a behavior modification program in Ensenada, Mexico. Unknown to them, the program was not at all what it advertised on its lovely brochure. There were no jet skis or outings to the beach. From age sixteen to eighteen, I was forced to live in deplorable conditions, eat terrible food, experience physical abuse (more times than I can remember), and not have any direct communication with my family. When I turned 18, the program had to release me. Two weeks after leaving, the program was closed by Mexican government officials for its subhuman conditions.

Once back home, I was so angry that I had been forced to go to this horrible place for so long. I vowed to get even with my parents and planned to do so by hurting myself. Off at college, I became involved in illegal activities and was eventually caught resulting in my entry to the judicial system. At the time, I knew I was only hurting myself, but in retrospect I can see my life was being guided. I had to complete three months of house arrest because of my crime. All I wanted to do was fight. The anger and hatred was more alive than ever. On my 20th birthday, my life was immersed in hatred. I punched a wall in my home that I thought was made of wood. It turned out the wood was only a façade covering a concrete wall. I broke my hand sending my knuckle through the bottom of my palm.

After surgery, still on house arrest, I felt more hate and anger than ever, still refused to accept responsibility for any of my actions. I decided it would be best for me to become a professional fighter. I learned the best fighters practiced Brazilian Jiu-Jitsu. The Jiu-Jitsu practitioners practiced yoga to improve their fighting ability and awareness. One night with a cast still affixed to my arm my mother introduced me to the practice of yogic deep breathing. Coming from such constant intense emotional states of frustration, anger, and hatred, the simple practice of focusing on elongating my breath blew my mind! It caused an immediate paradigm shift in my reality. Through the action of the breath, I found the ability to tune into my long lost parasympathetic nervous system. I instantly connected with an overwhelming sense of peace, tranquility, and serenity never known before. Thus, began my journey inward in search of spirit. Soon after, I began practicing yoga.

Mind you, I still adorn the government issue ankle monitor during the first few months of beginning yoga.

My life quickly changed. I did end up practicing martial arts earning countless national and world titles in very short succession. I began and quickly completed a college degree program. In relatively short time, I became certified to teach yoga, serving others and doing my part in making the world a better place.

I share this story to highlight how the suffering and hopelessness experienced during my teens led to the anger and hatred of my early adulthood. The passion to fight and harm led me to meditation and yoga. I first began the practices only to increase my ability to be violent and cause pain. Ironically, through the practice, I connected to my long lost true self and rediscovered my belief in God. There is a beautiful sermon written by Charles Haddon Spurgeon in the late 1800s in which he spoke of looking back at one's life and seeing two sets of footprints in the sand, ours and God's. Throughout the process, which continues to this day, the divine guided me through each step. In retrospect, I can see God walked with me step by step all throughout my journey, except through the hardest of times. During those times, there was only one set of footprints in the sand because He was carrying me, guiding me toward His will. That which I thought was destroying me, strengthened me. That which I thought would harden my heart, led me to soften my heart and allow it to overflow with love. My challenges were blessings in disguise. The loss of my self (ego) was the process of finding my true self and connecting to my outer purpose.

The inner purpose is everlasting and does not change. The inner purpose will always be the underlying principal behind all life. The outer purpose is in constant fluidity, which is why a heightened sense of presence is a prerequisite to realizing it.

Self-realization is the constant, unchanging permanent goal in life. Regarding outer purpose, one moment you may be a doctor, lawyer, realtor, secretary or any other profession when an intuitive realization or powerful synchronous experience presents itself. Following such intuition guides you toward purpose. Moments of synchronicity are meant to be perceived as road signs guiding you in the right direction. Synchronicity is divine guidance in the physical world.

When I decided to leave real estate, I did not have a great deal of money saved, but I knew opening the yoga studio was my purpose. I put all my resources into it. Three days before opening the studio my financial resources were exhausted. I was helping the construction crew with the finishing touches. The hardwood floors were almost completely installed. I owed them $3,100, which was due that evening. I went home for lunch and when I checked the mail, I found a letter from my insurance company. Enclosed was a check for a claim filed three years earlier that I had all but forgotten. The check totaled to $3,111!

When a person listens to that inner voice, the universe moves mountains to help him or her achieve the objective. Search deeply within. Follow the guidance you receive. When you know, you can accomplish your dreams, it is as if they are already a reality. Jesus reminded us, "Ask and it will be given to you, seek and you will find, knock and it will be opened to you."

Minor and Major Purpose

Another avenue for understanding purpose is by examining the stages of minor and major purpose. I encountered this philosophy through the teachings of Hazrat Inayat Khan in "Awakening of the Human Spirit".

The minor purpose teaches us the preeminent lessons needed early on to create the circumstances required to realize the major purpose later in life. The major purpose is the specific reason your spirit manifested into an individual being. The minor purpose is realized in the beginning of life. The major purpose is realized later in life as a culmination of all prior experiences.

There was a young thief who was not very successful in his trade. He went to a wise guru to ask for a blessing to be a better thief. The guru understood how the young man's minor purpose would prepare him for his greater purpose in life. He blessed the young man and encouraged him to find one or two more partners in crime. This would enable him to steal more. The guru's advice worked and the young man was more successful. With two partners in crime the young man increased his profits dramatically. He went back to the guru to thank him and ask for another blessing. The guru obliged and told him to form a group of 10 to really ramp up his profitability. The young man did as was suggested and reaped incredible benefits. He again went back to the guru who again blessed him and recommended he increase his group 10 to a band of 30. Profits increased three-fold. The cycle went on and on until the group the young man led numbered in the thousands. His financial success was unprecedented.

A tyrannical leader came into power, one that oppressed all the citizens and was very unjust. When asked for advice on how to handle the matter, the guru told the young man, he should lead his army of thieves to rise in revolution against the tyrannical leader. The group was successful in ousting the oppressive government, but before he could assume the leadership of the country, the young man passed away of an illness. The country held an election and chose the most appropriate leader to guide their country onward.

The young man would have done a fine job leading the entire country but that was not his major purpose. His major purpose was to restore justice to the land. He could only accomplish this purpose by first realizing his minor purpose. By being the great thief with the largest band of raiders, the young man was guided to accomplish his major purpose and create a lasting change for good on the planet.

In this manner, the minor purpose guides us to our major purpose in life. Sometimes early on in life, the lessons learned and strength gained from some not so admirable endeavors prove to be essential in achieving a much more noteworthy purpose. Whatever role you are playing in life, play it to the best of your ability. Martin Luther King Jr. said, "If a man is called to be a street sweeper, he should sweep the streets as Michelangelo painted or Beethoven composed music or Shakespeare wrote poetry. He should sweep streets so well that all the hosts of heaven and earth will pause to say, "Here lived a great street sweeper who did his job well."

You never know what your current position is preparing you for or guiding you toward, but you will only come to such an epiphany if you do your job so well the gates of heaven open so your efforts can be recognized and venerated.

Looking back at my life, I can clearly see how my minor purpose led and prepared me for my major purpose. Dealing with the suffering I experienced living my minor purpose prepared me for realizing my major purpose. In my minor purpose throughout the first 30 years of my life, I ran the emotional gauntlet using and selling drugs, and dealing with the ego that arose from being a successful martial artist. Amazingly enough drugs and fighting led me to begin my spiritual path through yoga. Through drugs, I found myself on house arrest. To become a better fighter, I was willing to try yoga and meditation. I thought drugs were the best way to escape the suffering inherent in life. Yoga and meditation were a much more effective means of tuning into peace.

I embraced this method because of the ineffectiveness of my drug use in solving the problem. Selling drugs helped me to better market and finance my teaching career (in the beginning stages). Learning to recover from martial arts injuries made me more capable to teach others how to heal themselves. Practicing yoga and meditation with a martial artists' fierce determination allowed me to go very far in these ancient practices. I practiced yoga and meditation like my life and physical well-being depended on it. More than that, I came to the realization my physical and emotional well-being depended on my spiritual practice. An unsavory minor purpose led me to a more meaningful major purpose of serving and guiding others on a path of peace. My minor purpose of selling drugs and fighting cumulatively led me right to this very moment writing these very words on this very page at this exact point in time. My hope is to inspire you to do your best, employ a gallant effort and realize your destiny. You may not understand the greater purpose at this moment but I promise there is one and you are knowingly or unconsciously working toward it.

    I did not see or appreciate the guiding light that directed me in my minor purpose. The universal order was always in progress whether I recognized or not. The things I learned as a young man allowed me to mature into a responsible, insightful adult capable of achieving his greater life's purpose and furthering the greater good in the world. This is the wisdom behind the minor and major purpose of life.

Individual and Collective Purpose

    Discussed earlier as inner and outer purpose, the individual purpose has two elements: to connect to a higher power within and to manifest that divine in the world around you. Everyone's individual purpose has the same ever important primary element of first reconnecting to source. First one must create a clear connection to their spirit so he or she may recognize the intuitive guidance that is always accessible. Next following that guidance in the spiritual life and the physical realm become the focus of one's energy. As individuals, we are all tied together to a greater cause. Individuals are all connected by an invisible energy that yokes, or binds, our existence into one single entity.

A single cell in the heart may feel that it operates entirely independently of all the other cells around it. The individual cell does not realize that it belongs to a community of cells that comprise the heart and facilitate blood circulating throughout the body. That single heart cell may perceive that it and another cell in the lungs have absolutely no connection as their shape, color, and function differ greatly. The cell in the lungs is part of a community that is part of the respiratory process in the body infusing blood with oxygen without which neither circulation nor life itself could exist. The cell in the heart and the cell in the lungs do not see their connection as individual entities in the collective of cells in the human body. Yet, the two different cells are entirely dependent on each other. The body could not survive without either the heart or the lungs.

Flying 1,000 miles into space, the planet could not be recognized to contain six billion individual human beings. It would only be perceived as one single entity, the planet earth. Unity or oneness is all a matter of perspective.

The collective consciousness of humanity has a greater purpose and everyone plays a unique role. You may not see how your life and individual purpose touches the life and purpose of another seemingly unconnected individual across the globe from your humble perspective. In one way or another your thoughts and actions influence every other person in the planet. Inversely, this paradox is true when describing the collective reflection everyone else in the planet has on you. As the collective conscious raises its vibration, individuals will become more aware of their specific part in the whole, the harmony on the planet will increase as we work toward arriving at the golden age of peace, love, and abundance.

There is an interesting true story that takes place on a small island near Japan. A group of indigenous monkeys would eat sweet potatoes they found on the beach. The problem was that the beach sand covered the potatoes and ruined the experience the monkeys had eating their favorite food. One day, a single monkey figured out he could wash the sand off the potatoes in the ocean and enjoy his food without the grittiness of sand between his teeth. Another saw the process and began to imitate him. Not long after 10 or so of the monkeys began to mimic the original primate. Once a point of critical mass was achieved all the monkeys started washing their potatoes off in the ocean. Scientists noticed what was happening and were amazed to discover on another island with no contact hundreds of miles away, the monkeys spontaneously began washing their potatoes off in the ocean. The occurrence serves as a documented example of the unseen metaphysical connection between all life that is beyond the understanding of the physical mind. This is the subject matter of what science coins' quantum theory.

The ancient mystics have understood the existence of the underlying connection between all life for eons. In physics, the study of molecules demonstrates this same principle and is known as phase transition. When a certain number of molecules line up in an atom and the critical mass is reached, all the rest of the molecules align in the same formation and the composition of the atom transforms.

I described this process because in this manner, a spiritual revolutionary can inspire and unite the collective mind and impact the world. The collective consciousness is the most powerful force of unity on the planet. What is the collective purpose? In a sense, the collective purpose has the same intention as the individual purpose: to leave the world a better place than we found it. War is and for millennia has been far too common throughout the globe. When a certain number of individuals choose to stand up for peace this number for critical mass will be met and everyone's value systems will fall in alignment. The need, desire, and ultimately the motivation for war will disappear. When the collective stands to improve the environment even at the prospect of personal discomfort, the industrial practices damaging nature will cease. There will be nature reserves, a greater supply of clean water, greater numbers and diversity of wildlife, and larger forests across the globe. The collective will find the unifying power to restore the planet to its pristine state and leave the world a better place than we inherited it.

The Native American culture has a tradition of considering the well-being of the next seven generations when making important decisions. When enough individuals utilize this way of thinking, the collective understanding of how to create a better future will transform and save the world. Together we can make a change and unite our purpose procuring the ability to support life on this planet for many generations. The most exciting aspect of this way of thinking is that it all starts with you! And it begins right now in your heart at this very moment. Together we can change the world. There is no time like the present. The time to begin manifesting a better future is today.

Remember to be for what you want instead of against what you do not want. If you want to end drug use, be for sobriety not against drugs. If you want to support a better environment be for the sanctity of nature not against pollution. During the Vietnam War Era Mother Theresa was invited to an anti-war protest. She declined but told the protestors she would be willing to attend a rally for peace. Transforming your way of thinking not only changes your life, but also the world around you. What you think, you create.

In this manner, we stop building more dams to hold back the flow of the river of non-working thinking. This is how we change the direction of the flow of the water. When I am against war, all my thoughts are based on war and the harm it causes. Thinking this way can only lead to continuing the practice of fighting. By changing my entire outlook on the matter, I serve as an example for others to follow. By supporting peace, I create the mental images of what a peaceful planet would be like and can clearly see the steps needed to take to realize this dream. Be for what you want instead of against what you do not want. This way you become an active, productive part in the process of achieving the change you desire. Like Gandhi said, "Be the change you want to see in the world".

    Overcoming the pseudo soul more commonly known as the ego is the most important obstacle mankind collectively confronts today. The empowerment of the ego has misguided our spiritually aimed religions and transformed these sacred traditions into little more than cultural phenomena showcasing the importance of external appearances in our society. Many people attend churches, mosques, and synagogues to be seen preforming the act instead of devotionally practicing spirituality.

    For many, Christianity has become "churchianity," Judaism has become "synagogism," and Islam has become "mosqulam". There are those in our society who maintain a religious practice for appearance sake. They make a big deal about praying in public where they can be seen praying. Internally experiencing the truth is the method to disempowering the ego and to realize the intention of the masters was to rediscover the soul. Rather than proclaim allegiance a specific religion, act as Jesus acted. Learn to practice compassion and forgiveness. Better yet, cease judgment and blame altogether. Then the need to forgive disappears entirely. If as a society, we collectively practiced these principles in our affairs, there would be no more wars, no more prisons, no more crime, and no need for law enforcement. The Tao Te Ching teaches that when one requires rules to be virtuous, virtue is not possible. This path guides the collective to experience a revival of truth within. The resurrection of Christ would take place in the heart of every individual who learns to connect to the Christ Consciousness within.

One thousand churches, mosques and synagogues pale in comparison to the power of light and love found in the temple of a soul with a pure heart. Through meditation, this level of consciousness is accessible. Through indomitable devotion and dedication, the external manifestation of the internal reality is possible. I know as I have witnessed this force in action on many occasions through the examples of my spiritual teachers and by overcoming obstacles in my own life. Regarding obstacles, let me give you the most powerful secret. Surrender is the key to accessing your true inner power. Nonviolence in the face of aggression will always prevail through the most unlikely of means. Gandhi, Martin Luther King Jr., and Nelson Mandela are all shining examples of the power of peace, love, devotion, and non-violence. They embodied the teachings of the ancient spiritual masters and you have this capability.

Let nothing disturb your peace. Become resolute to love. Renounce all forms of violence. Dedicate your life to the service of others. These are the guidelines to living your spiritual potential. Live each moment in the present and you will spread the loving light of awareness to all you encounter. Global transformation is possible. The proving ground for the transformation of our society lies in the canvas of your heart. With your meditation, paint a devotional masterpiece. Unlike the world of Michelangelo or Da Vinci, this masterful work of the heart is for no one other than the Self. It is the source of divinity within you.

People tell me, "It's not realistic to act or live that way". I say to them, this is the only way to live. My body is only a temporary storage space for the soul. You may be a teacher, a doctor, a lawyer, or even an inmate, but only for the time being. You have the power to choose to identify with an impermanent source of existence or with the soul. With proper identification of reality, the bureaucratic deferring of right action ceases. You become empowered to act righteously on your own accord as you are acting from your true nature and not relying on the decision or judgments of anyone or anything outside yourself.

The term holy war is a defilement to all that is celestial. Blind belief in religious dogma has caused an indescribable amount of pain and suffering throughout the ages. An untold number of people have been killed from any number of religious military campaigns (talk about an oxymoron) from the inquisitions, to the holocaust, to the jihad today in the Middle East. Blind acceptance of religious principle is just as senseless as not believing in God at all. In either route, there is an apparent lack of divine guidance in the life of both non-believer and the dogmatic extremist. Paramahansa Yogananda said, "God never punishes man for not believing in Him, man punishes himself. If one does not believe in the dynamo and cuts the wires that connect his home to that source, he forfeits the advantages of that electrical power. Likewise, to disavow the Intelligence that is omnipresent in all creation is to deny the conscious link with the Source of divine wisdom and love that empowers the process of ascension in Spirit."

Belief alone is not enough to bring about transformation. A strong conviction is required to maintain the intensity of spiritual practice required to lead the individual to the actual experience of God. Only in this experience can the individual come to embody a truth manifested through divine guidance. Belief without experience is dangerous and allows individuals to be controlled and manipulated to do terrible things. The actual experience of the spiritual being is empowered by the strongest force in the universe. Meditation is the process that guides one to such an experience.

Here I will introduce you to the most basic form of meditation that also served as my introduction to the practice. There are an infinite number of types of meditation. You must find which one works best for you. Stick with one type of meditation and avoid changing methods unless necessary or you are guided to do so by your teacher. The method should be simple but will require effort. Training the mind to focus its concentrative energy requires discipline and may be a skill with which you are unfamiliar. Patience is your best tool in this field. Consistency is your next best tool. With practice, you will create results. It all starts by tuning awareness into the breath.

Breath Meditation

Start by sitting up straight in a chair or seated cross-legged on the floor.

Close your eyes and begin to tune into your breathing.

Focus on the quality of your inhales and exhales.

When you catch your mind wandering bring your focus back to your breath.

You will not stop the noise outside yourself; just bring your focus back to the breath.

Don't judge yourself, your thoughts, or anyone else around you. Just focus on the breath.

Pay attention to the rise of your stomach as you inhale and the fall the stomach as you exhale. As thoughts come up, let them go.

Bring your awareness back to the breath. Continue inhaling and exhaling.

Take three more deep breaths and slowly begin to open your eyes.

Chapter 2: Spiritual Energy

"Our life is shaped by our mind. We become what we think"
–The Buddha

All thoughts, feelings, and emotions are the vibrational expressions of the divine voice in you. The matter of the mind is spiritual energy manifest. An individual's frequency is the level of clarity at which the divine signal is being transmitted. All life is the culmination of cosmic vibration. By learning how to heighten your frequency, you gain the ability to heighten the quality of reception of your signal. We are a microcosm for the macrocosm to operate through. Increasing the intensity of your vibrational field allows you to increase your effect on the world around you.

Utilizing spiritual technology (in the form of some spiritual discipline) is an opportunity to heighten your personal vibration and influence the world. Bringing awareness to the frequency fluctuations of consciousness attunes us to the process of elevating or lowering the quality of our connection. Take for example watching television. If you are watching a violent show you are being negatively affected. Your spiritual frequency is being lowered. Your option is to change the channel or turn the TV off altogether.

While in conversation with a cynical person your tone is negatively influenced. It is your prerogative to inject that conversation with a sense of gratitude raising the level of both your and the other person's frequency.

I remember asking my teacher, Yogi Shivraj, how to heighten my spiritual vibration. He had a very common answer to all my questions. After a while I knew what he was going to say before he said it, "Meditate". Meditation seems to be the answer to all my questions and the solutions to all my problems. I found the solution to raising my frequency. With Yogi Ji, I did a great deal of mantra meditation. A mantra is a sacred syllable or set of syllables that when chanted internally or out loud heightens the spiritual frequency. I have often heard mantras defined as a formula, a method of divine communication. There are an infinite number of different mantras, which should be prescribed to you individually by a master. Often these mantras are esoteric or secret teachings that should not be shared with anyone else. A chanting practice you can begin on your own would be to chant the world *"aum"* aloud. Do this with your eyes closed. Focus in on the quality of vibration in you. After sometime (five to ten minutes) chant the mantra silently in your mind. Finish the practice with a moment of silence. By tuning into the universal vibration (represented by the word aum), you will be able to harmonize and heighten your own vibration.

Mantras

An ancient yogic text named the "Shvetashvara Upanishad" beautifully describes the power of the mantra in the 1st chapter, verses 13-14 (Easwaran, The Upanishads, 1987):

Fire is not seen until one fire stick rubs against another, though the fire remains hidden in the fire stick. So does the Lord remain hidden in the body until He is revealed through the mystic mantra.

Let your body be the lower fire stick; let the mantra be the upper. Rub them against each other in meditation and realize the Lord.

If chanting aum is not your thing and you do not have a spiritual guide, you can choose another mantra that resonates with you. All religions have their own mantras. Christianity uses the name *Jesus* Christ or the Lord's Prayer chanted repetitively as a mantra. St. Francis chanted, *My God, My All*. Catholicism uses *Hail Mary* as a mantra. A Jewish mantra is *Baruch Atah*

Adonai, means, "blessed be thou oh Lord of the universe". Islam uses *Bismillah ir-Rahman ir-Rahim,* which translates to "in the name of Allah, the merciful, the compassionate" or even *Allah.*

There is an infinite number of Hindu mantras. One example is the mantra Gandhi used to chant *Rama,* which represents one of the many names of God in Hinduism. Another popular mantra using this name is *Hare Rama Hare Rama, Rama Rama Hare Hare, Hare Krishna Hare Krishna, Krishna Krishna Hare Hare.* A mantra I use with great success is a chant to Shiva the lord of yoga, *Om Nama Shivaya meaning, "I* bow to Shiva". The most common Buddhist mantra is *Om Mani Padme Om,* which means "the jewel in the heart of the lotus". Do some research and find a mantra that resonates with you.

For those who do not feel comfortable with the idea of a manifest God, *aum* is a great mantra because it represents the un-manifested or impersonal representation of the divine. When saying aum the A stands for the waking state. The U stands for the dreaming state. M stands for the dreamless state. Together AUM represents the supreme state of divine union. This is the an extremely powerful mantra chanted by countless individuals over the millennia

Using a single word that represents a great ideal such as *peace* or *love* works best for some. I recommend using a mantra that has been used before by others for a spiritual practice, as there is great strength to be discovered in utilizing the collective consciousness. Once you have chosen your mantra, try to stick with it and not change mantras. When digging a well for water, if you keep changing location and digging new holes you will never find water. As with a mantra, if you keep changing mantras, you will never reach the source (Easwaran, The Mantram Hankbook, 2009).

Chakras

Every spiritual discipline has a different term to describe the energy that flows through us. Western religions describe this energy as Spirit. Eastern sources have used the term Prana, Chi, or Tao. Ayurveda practices define a system of channels and blockages called *nadi's and granthi's.* Acupuncturists refers to these systems as meridians and pressure points.

The chakras are major energy centers that operate as transformers to manifest spiritual energy in to physical attributes. The word chakra means, "wheel". There are seven chakras, each with its own qualities. I will describe them here briefly.

The first chakra is known as the root chakra and is associated with the color red. This chakra is at the base of our spine below the sexual organs. It deals with traits related to survival.

The second chakra is associated with the color orange. It is located in the area of the sexual organs. It deals with matters of pleasure both sexual and material. Our desires are the concern of the second chakra.

The third chakra is known for the color yellow. It is around the navel. The third chakra is associated with issues of power.

The fourth chakra is the heart chakra. It is associated with green and can be found in the center of the chest. The heart chakra manifests the ideals of compassion, love, and gratitude. The heart chakra separates the three lower primal chakras from the three higher spiritual centers.

The fifth chakra is located in the throat. It is known by the color blue. The fifth chakra is the center for manifesting creativity.

The sixth chakra is known as the third eye. It is located between the eyebrows. It is specifically associated with functions of the pineal gland. The color for the sixth chakra is indigo or dark blue. The third eye is where our intuition is manifested.

The seventh chakra is known as the crown chakra and is located at the top of the head. Its color is violet (or white in some traditions). The crown chakra is the center of our spirituality.

When unbalanced, we manifest the negative traits of each chakra. When in balance we express life through the positive traits of each chakra. Since at our source we are energy, it is easier to create lasting change in life first by changing our energy instead of externally trying to modify our behavior or external circumstances. The chakras can be experienced individually, but were designed to function in balance together as a complete model.

The chakras operate as organs of our metaphysical anatomy. Imagine our metaphysical body functions like a radio tower. Each chakra represents a section of the tower used to materialize the divine signal. The more balanced we are, the clearer the transmission of the signal becomes. If you are interested in studying the chakras in greater depth, there is a vast amount of literature available. I recommend reading the works of David Pond if you are attracted to studying the chakras (Pond, 1999).

Chakra Characteristics

Number	*Sanskrit Name*	*Color*	*Location*	*Quality*	*Mantra*
1	Muladhara	Red	Base of spine	Survival	Lam
2	Svadisthana	Orange	Sexual organs	Pleasure	Vam

3	Manipura	Yellow	Navel	Power	Ram
4	Anahata	Green	Chest	Love	Yam
5	Vishudda	Blue	Throat	Creativity	Ham
6	Ajna	Indigo	Brow	Intuition	Shyam
7	Sahasara	Violet	Crown of the head	Spirituality	Om

Chakra Meditation

Begin to focus on your breathing. Pay attention to your inhaling and exhaling. When you catch you mind wandering bring your focus back to the breath. Watch how as you inhale your stomach rises and as you exhale your stomach falls. Once you have become centered, you can begin working with the chakras.

Imagine a red light entering your body through the crown of your head on an inhale and traveling down to the base of your spine. As you exhale, follow that red light back up through the top of your head. Take three breaths this way.

Now watch as an orange light enters your head and travels down through your body to your sexual organs. And back up through the top of the head on an exhale. Take three breaths this way.

Watch a yellow light enter your body through the head and move down to the navel on an inhale and back up to the head on an exhale. Take three breaths this way.

Now observe a green light enter your head and move down to the center of your chest on an inhale. Follow the energy back up to the head on an exhale. Take three breaths this way.

Watch as a blue light enters the head and travels down to the throat on an inhale and as you exhale follow that light back up to your head. Take three breaths this way.

> Observe an indigo or dark blue colored light entering the crown of your head and traveling down between your eye brows on an inhale and back out the crown of the head on an exhale. Take three breaths here.
>
> Breath in a violet colored light in the crown of your head on an inhale and exhale the light back out on an exhale. Take three breaths this way.
>
> Now come back to your normal breathing just inhaling and exhaling naturally. Take three more breaths and when you are ready begin to open your eyes.

Practicing this meditation helps to align and harmonize the chakras. We are energy first and matter second. Wise men have said that we are spiritual beings having a human experience. To change the world outside of ourselves we first must transform our inner world. Balancing the chakras using this meditation is a powerful method to ring harmony to all aspects of your life. Use this technique in the morning, during the day, or before going to sleep and you will experience a greater balance in your life. You can perform this practice anytime you feel out of balance energetically and want to do something to harmonize and heighten your vibration. You have the power to create change in your life at any moment by tuning your focus inside and connecting with the innate energy system operating on a metaphysical level within you. It only takes a few minutes to tune in. Give yourself the greatest gift of peace and tranquility that can only be uncovered through meditation.

Frequency

The important concept to understand is that our life's energy can be transformed from a lower frequency to a higher more divine vibration. Before we discuss more tools to heighten frequency, first let's cover the general levels of vibration. The energy we are covering may include but not specifically refer to your level of physical energy.

Your energy field is determined by your Spirit, Prana, or Chi. Everything in existence is in constant vibration. Molecules whether in a solid, liquid or gaseous state are in constant movement. In terms of our spiritual frequency, the faster the movement of the vibration, the more you move in the direction of spirit. The slower the movement of the vibration, the closer to the material world of problems you navigate toward. You have the ability to discern that what lowers and heightens the frequency of your energy field. Gravitate toward that which heightens your energy. Positive people, spiritual literature and spending time in nature are examples of energy heightening experiences. Violent movies, unhealthy food, drugs and alcohol are examples of things that lower your frequency.

In his book "Spiritual Solutions for All Your Problems", Wayne Dyer describes vibrational frequencies in our energy field. He uses three levels to differentiate between types of spiritual frequencies. I will label three levels of energy from slowest to fastest: low-level, mid-level and high-level frequencies.

Low-level frequency is the state of ego consciousness. We experience illness, disharmony, fear, stress, anxiety, and tend to get stuck living in the past or future most the time. Midlevel frequency energy is the state of group consciousness. We do not experience extensive negative symptoms and tend to associate ourselves with feeling ok or just average.

Living in a high-level energy field, we experience God consciousness. This can also be described as Christ consciousness, Buddhahood, or self-realization. You experience unity with God. Your health is perfect. Your desires have merged with the desires of the divine will. You see the world as one organism and have lifted the veil of illusion in your heart (Dyer W., There's A Spiritual Solution To Every Problem, 2001).

Here I must mention Patanjali's second sutra, which is discussed in greater detail later in this book. **Yoga (union) is the cessation of the fluctuations of the mind.** Even 5,000 years ago, Patanjali knew about these vibrations.

When we speed up a frequency infinitesimally it looks like a straight line. Reaching a point of union or God consciousness, the fluctuations of frequency become so high; they appear to stop all together. The stream of divine signal is at such a high state the message is completely clear. You heighten your frequency with your spiritual practice. Like Yogi Ji said, in meditation we find the answer to all things. With meditation, we learn to elevate our consciousness from the real of the senses to the realm of the spirit. We move from the darkness of ignorance to the light of awareness.

In our society, people seem to be stuck in their lower chakras. The lower chakras represent our basic survival needs, pleasure, and power. To raise our frequency, it is essential to shift awareness to the higher chakras. These energy centers represent love, creativity, intuition, and spirituality. Take this opportunity to distinguish whether you tend to operate in the lower or higher chakras most the time in your own life.

Just because we are in a human body does not mean we are human beings. Most people tend to be driven by animal-like survival and sexual instincts. Shift your awareness to higher levels of thought to live more in your higher energy centers. Ask yourself what music or television you watch that encourages you to get stuck in these lower energy centers? What are most of your conversations about? What spiritual practices have you experienced that raised your awareness? That which we think in our minds, we attract to our lives. Here, I will refer to the quote by Buddha at the beginning of the chapter. The quote begins the Dhammapada:

Our life is shaped by our mind; we become what we think. Suffering follows an evil thought as the wheels of a cart follow the oxen that draw it.

Our life is shaped by our mind; we become what we think. Joy follows a pure thought like a shadow that never leaves.

Raise your vibration by shifting your focus. Merge your will with the will of the divine and you will discover your truest nature.

Chapter 3: Frequencies of the Heart: Love, Compassion and Gratitude

"When I speak of love I am not speaking of some sentimental and weak response. I am speaking of that force which all of the great religions have seen as the supreme unifying principal of life. Love is somehow the key that unlocks the door which leads us to ultimate reality." -Martin Luther King Jr.

Love

The language of God has no words. Love is the allpowerful form of divine communication. Through thick and thin, through highs and lows, love stays consistent. Through the emotional ups and downs experienced in life, love brings a cessation to such fluctuations with understanding. The yin yang sign has a black side and a white side. Love sees the beauty by understanding the entire symbol. Without the darkness, light could never be so bright. Without bad, good would not matter. Without the hideous, beauty would not be so attractive. Unconditional love knows no bound, as its understanding is complete.

I will paraphrase "The Book of Mirdad" by Mikhail Naimy. If you were to focus all your love on one leaf in a tree, how could you not also love the branches that attach and feed the leaf? You would also love the trunk that created the branches, the bark that protects the trunk, the sap that acts as the lifeline of the tree, roots that nourish the sap, the soil that holds firm the roots, the air, sun, and water that make the soil fertile. This is the tree of life. Love for the single leaf cannot be separated from a love for the entire tree.

You are the tree of life. Now imagine yourself being the tree, but the tree is upside down. Your rots are in heaven. The leaves, flowers, and fruits of your heavenly body manifest here on earth. You and all your actions are a divine manifestation of God, of Love.

Recognize the good could not exist without the bad. The beautiful could not exist without that which is ugly. The wilted and withered fruit gave its strength and beauty so the ripe delicious fruit could flourish. Instead of cursing the withered fruit, love it for what it is. Imperfection is the martyr for perfection. Hate is the repression of love. Hate is a poison to the cursed and he who curses. Recognizing ignorance is humbling. A river doesn't know it flows to the ocean. But when it realizes this truth, it discovers the ocean replenishes the river.

Love is a blessing to both the beloved and the devotee. The relationship between a disciple and a Guru is one of true divinity. The all-knowing Guru blesses his devotee with wisdom, energetic transmission, and de-hypnotization. The devotee (shishya) is the best role to play. It is even better than the Guru. To follow your heart, to truly know is to become a drop of water. Rumi wrote, "You are not a drop in the ocean. You are the ocean in a drop." The love that can only be realized in presence will flow from your essential being-ness like water from a fountain.

Recognizing instances of ignorance in my life has been the most humbling experience. When you break down the word Guru: gu means light, ru means dark. The word guru describes the ability to turn light into dark. The Guru turns ignorance into awareness is the one who reunites us with our true self. The relationship between romantic partners is not necessarily love. The way parents love a child is on the path to real love. Devotion to the Guru is the key, the lock, and the doorway to the heart.

A mountain stream is ignorant of its true destination, its unity with all things. The stream unites with other streams on its journey becoming a river ultimately merging in to the sea. The sea replenishes the stream by transforming into rain through photosynthesis allowing the natural cycle to take place. The spiritual teacher is the gravity that unites the ignorant stream with the sea of awareness. The highs, the lows, the ignorance and awareness, when you understand the big picture you see every part of the process is guided by love. Love is in all and all is love.

Love and Fear

The divine umbrella covers all things in this universe. Everything has its place in the realm of the ethereal. Rumi wrote, "There is a place beyond the good and the bad, I will meet you there". God is in all things in creation. When we overcome the illusion of duality, we see there is no good or bad, no right or wrong. There just is. The Bible says, "I am that I am" and in your truest nature you are divine.

Since all things are under God's umbrella, all vibrations are spiritual. The only difference is their level of frequency. What is the level of your frequency? What do you do that raises or lowers your spiritual vibration?

Love and fear are the same energy merely moving in the opposite direction. Osho teaches that love opens, fears closes. Love expands, while fear shrinks. Love allows you to trust, while fear creates doubt. When you practice meditation, you learn to lose yourself in love. When you live in fear, you lose yourself in anxiety.

Love and fear cannot exist simultaneously, because they are the same form of energy merely at the opposite ends of the spectrum. The Bible supports this idea in John 4:18, "There is no fear in love; but perfect love casts our fear, because fear involves torment, but he who fears has not been made perfect as love." The Bible goes as far as saying "God is love". God's love is indivisible. The divine cannot be broken down or separated into different parts. It cannot be divided.

The spirit is in all and all is in the spirit. Only love, not fear, exists in the divine realm.

If love and fear are the same energy, why do we feel so differently when we experience the two emotions? Fear comes about when our spiritual vibrations are at their lowest frequency. We experience love when our frequency is at its highest. Fear is a lack of love, and changes the direction of the energy inside us. To transform fear into love requires courage. To be courageous is to be steadfast in faith regardless of fluctuations in emotional states. Surrender to your fears as a means of embracing love.

Courage does not mean that you do not have fear. Courage is the presence of fear and consciously deciding to move forward despite the potential risks. Courage is having faith in the understanding of the divine order of the universe and acting accordingly.

Courage and bravery are two very different things. Most people think they are the same thing, but they have one very important differentiating factor, fear. Bravery is the ability to confront pain, danger or acts of intimidation without any impression of fear. Strength in character enables a person to always seem bigger than the catastrophe at hand, regardless if he is more powerful or lesser than what he is facing. An example is David facing Goliath in the Bible. David felt no fear leading up to the climactic moment because he knew he could easily kill Goliath without even coming close to the giant. His bravery was the main theme of the story.

An example of courage would be a soldier trying to break out of a POW camp. He would be killed if he was caught but love for family would allow him to find the courage to attempt the dangerous feat. Fear gives us insight into potential pitfalls that can only be avoided with the presence of fear. Courage requires critical thinking. In a situation where a person is brave he may seem bigger than he really is. These qualities are normally developed due to the society or families values an individual is exposed to. Bravery can be maintained without a cause; courage is powered by its cause that could be from love, devotion, friendship, compassion or some other altruistic value.

Courage depends on faith and understanding. Life really starts when you have the courage to move into the unknown. Following the heart often takes you down an unstable, insecure road. But when following the heart, there is faith and in faith there is understanding. This is the way of courage.

An uncomfortable byproduct of love is vulnerability. To love another, you must be totally willing to be hurt. Your heart must be wide open. When you are in fear, the heart is closed, because you are worried about being hurt. To love you must be courageous and being willing to be hurt. You say to yourself, "Yes I may be hurt by opening my heart to this person, but the chance to be in love is more important than the potential of being hurt." Being courageous is how you change course on the road between fear and love.

Many organized religions use fear to force obedience. At a very young age, I had a hard time believing an all-loving God could send his children to suffer in hell for the rest of eternity. In maturity, I have learned hell does not exist in the afterlife. Heaven and hell exist in the here and now and are created by the way we chose to perceive our experience of life. If you think things are horrible and will never improve, you are living in hell. If you instead chose to believe in the order of the universe and know every moment is divine, you are living in heaven. The next time someone asks you, "How are you?" respond by saying, "I am blessed". And you truly will be blessed!

It is wrong for anyone (governments, religious teachers, family member etc.) to use fear to manipulate us into a desired reaction. Religions are cultural collections of spiritual techniques. The religions of the world are wonderful in their intention. It is when individuals or entities use fear in the context of religion to control that evil is given a breeding ground. Lose your attachment to religious titles. Experiment with different techniques from all religions to find which ones work best for you. There are many ways to communicate. You can send a letter, email, and make a phone call, text, videoconference. The list goes on and on. Different religious practices have unique methods of spiritual technology. You should try them all to find out which form of divine communication works best for you. Forget the label and focus on the intention and more importantly the results. It could be counting mala beads, using a mantra, saying Hail Mary's with a rosary, gazing into a fire, standing on your head, praying, meditating or any of the plethora of practices available. Try as many spiritual practices as you can and use the techniques that are most effective at creating a space of divine communication for you. The goal is to commune with God. Find the technique(s) that allows you to lose yourself in love and run with it. Search deeply, practice heroically and you will find what you are looking. Soon you will discover the self. God is in you and always has been.

Clarifying Perspective

Different religions across the globe may seem to have many unique characteristics and traditions on the outside. Despite their differences, each religion maintains the same goal, for the practitioner to experience divine communion, to realize God. Whether it be a Mohammedan bowing toward Mecca five times a day, a Jew reading Torah, a Hindu chanting a mantra with mala beads, a Buddhist meditating in silence, or a Christian praying to Christ, the goal of each of these forms of spiritual technology is to commune with God. Until the practitioner dissolves the illusionary veil separating himself from truth, earnest effort, consistent devotion, and unswerving faith are prerequisites.

Shri Ramakrishna told a story about four blind men happening upon an elephant in the jungle. The first man grabbed the elephant's trunk and exclaimed he was holding a club. The next man touched a leg and concluded it was a tree stump. The third blind man touch the elephant's belly and knew his hands lay on a water pot. The fourth man took hold of an ear and described to the others he was holding a basket.

A man walked upon the scene and explained to the four blind men that they were not grasping separate entities. There was no club, tree stump, water pot, or basket. The four blind men were all holding onto the same elephant.

Each religion on earth guides its followers to take hold of the divine by one means or another. Each religion has a different name for God. Maybe they call Him God, Allah, Jesus, Krishna, Buddha, Yahweh, or any other manifested incarnation of God. But every religious practitioner is reaching toward and grasping onto the same source of divinity. An understanding of the truth is realized by internalizing the teachings of a true spiritual master. The specific name of the tradition, religion, or master is inconsequential. What really matters is the truth. We all begin the spiritual journey with closed eyes, not knowing what we are grasping for in the dark. The light of awareness is the underlying truth behind all reality. With dedication, your eyes will open to the connection behind all existence and you, too, will experience the divine communion I am writing about.

When life gives you lemons, make lemonade. We associate certain circumstances in life with great pain, suffering, or unhappiness. It may be the ending of a relationship, the death of a loved one, the loss of a job, a financial difficulty, or any other insurmountable hurdle. Perhaps you are just grasping a club, tree stump, water pot, or basket. These struggles are a form of celestial guidance. When we accept our struggles, and embrace our suffering, life becomes effortless and easy. We recognize the purpose behind each challenge.

In its 68th verse, the Tao Te Ching states, "Whatever I fight weakens me. What I cooperate with strengthens me." Do not fight that which appears to be a great impediment in your life. Rather, embrace the opportunities hidden in each challenge. In this way, you realize your destiny. Resolve to give up your peace for no individual situation or perceived setback. Everything that happens is part of a larger plan. Embrace all aspects of your life by seeing God in every person and everything. Nothing is out of place. You are exactly where you are supposed to be, right here right now.

Accept your difficulties. Coming to a place of appreciation for all challenges allows life to flow seamlessly. By mastering our mind, we master the art of living. Neither good nor bad exist. God is behind all things. Ascend separation and recognize the unifying force behind all life.

The way a gemstone is cut allows for each portion of the gem to reflect light. Whether the stone is hand-cut or lasercut does not matter in terms of the reflection of light. The size and angle of the cut is inconsequential in refracting light to and from every direction. So too do all things in existence operate as a reflection of the light within. The Almighty reflects in all matter in creation. The individual who realizes the self sees the creator reflected in every particle. Everything is sacred. Even that which seems to be impure serves a purpose. Living this principle, you develop an appreciation for all life and become an active participant in the reflection of peace, truth and light. Maintain a gemstone's view of the world. Receive and reflect from and to all in the world.

Qualities of Love

All love is not the same. The love most of us relate to when we hear the word love is some type of conditioned love. The highest level of love is unconditional love. To experience the peak of love, we do not have to climb to a mountaintop. All we need do is get out of the way and allow ourselves to receive what has been there all along.

In the 21st chapter of the book of John, Christ teaches a powerful lesson about the quality of love. He asks Peter three times, "Do you love me?" Peter becomes more and more frustrated with each repetition of the question replying, "Yes Lord you know I love you." The English version of this account loses much in translation. The New Testament was written mostly in Greek. Each time Jesus asks Peter the question, he uses different words to denote the varying qualities of love.

The first two times Jesus asks the question he uses the word "agape," which translates as unconditional or divine love. Peter replies using the word "phileo" for love. Phileo denotes brotherly love. The third-time Christ asks the question he uses the word "phileo" in an attempt to educate Peter in the subtle nuances of the qualities of love and to demonstrate the supreme quality of love needed to carry on the message after his passing. Peter replies a third time, "Lord, you know everything; you know that I love you," finally using the word "agape".

There are four qualities of love described in the Greek language: Eros, Phileo, Storge, and Agape.

The first level of love is eros. This term describes the way romantic lovers feel in the early stages of a relationship. This is a powerful level of love but based on condition. Would we feel this strongly about the other if they were not our lover? The fact is we loving him or her because we are in a relationship. I know we are getting rather philosophical here, but this train of thought begins to beg the question, "What is unconditional love"?

The second level of love you are likely familiar with is phileo. This is where we get the name for the city of Philadelphia, the city of brotherly love. Phileo as mentioned before represents friendship or brotherly love. This could be used to describe the level at which life longtime friends care for each other, a sibling loves another sibling, or the way a lifelong time lover feels about one another. This love, although a valid level of love is based on condition. If the other person was a friend, brother, or spouse would you love them the same? The condition is the comradery you share with this person. At this idea, you may balk and say, I love my friends unconditionally. Ask yourself, if they were not your friends would you love them the same way? The condition is that they are your friends.

Another degree of love is storge. This term represents familial love. It describes the way a mother loves a child, a daughter loves a father, and the depth a grandparent loves his or her grandchildren. The condition is created with the strong force of family relationship. The love would not be the same if the child were not your child.

The pinnacle of love is agape. The term is defined in the dictionary as unconditional love. The true meaning of the word agape can only be understood as God's love for us. God's love is based on no conditions because God is love. The way God loves us is entirely unconditional. No matter what we do, how good or how bad of a decision we make, God continues loving us. Divine love is absolute. In his lesson, Christ attempted to teach Peter the ultimate love needed to spread the light of awareness throughout the world, an unbound, overflowing, and unconditional love.

The fact Christ attempted to teach one of his students how to love in the degree of agape love encourages us that we are capable of such divinity in our own hearts. You may be asking yourself "How is it possible to learn to love the way God loves us?" This happens when we overcome the idea of separation, the notion of duality. You and God are not two but one. Ascending beyond the ego, the sense of a separate self, this idea of I, me, and mine, we come to the realization of the true self. In our quintessential nature, we are divine. The early 20th century Jesuit priest Pierre Teilhard de Chardin beautifully stated, "You are not a human being having a spiritual experience. You are a spiritual being having a human experience".

You are divine and your purpose is to fulfill God's work, to complete his divine mission. You are entirely capable of living in agape love, the unconditional receptivity to your omnipresent state of blessing. When you allow yourself to be open to receiving divine love, you gain the ability to reflect that love in the world. Think about what it would feel like to love everyone and everything the way God loves you. The capability is in you. In you is such a glorious potential. Get lost in this love and you will find your authentic self. You are love and when you come to embody this reality you will come to recognize your true self. Like the Beatles sang "All You Need Is Love". In truth, all you *are* is love, revel in your magnificence. Love deeply in agape love.

Paramahansa Yogananda's teacher Sri Yukteswar spoke of love, "Ordinary love is selfish, darkly rooted in desires and satisfactions. Divine love is without condition, without boundary, without change. The flux of the human heart is gone forever at the transfixing touch of pure love."

Gratitude

The dictionary defines gratitude as "thankfulness". The practical application of the word is much more meaningful than the definition infers. It is the sense of appreciation experienced relative to momentary circumstances. At this exact moment, are you aware and appreciative of all the universe continuously creates for us? We are given many blessings in disguise. What often looks at first like a curse or a setback turns out to be a blessing. Knowing that our lives are guided by an infinite intelligence allows us to recognize there is a purpose in all things even if we cannot see what that purpose is from our humble point of view. Gratitude is a shift in perspective that can transform our outlook from hopelessness to harmoniousness.

Learning how to cultivate gratitude in our lives when we are feeling down is an essential skill for all spiritual aspirants. It allows us to make the change needed to see the glass half full instead of half empty. When we become grateful for that emptiness, it allows God to fill that void with peace and understanding. If the glass were always full how could it ever be filled? The sensation of need is the opportunity to receive direction from the universal will. God's purpose is to provide for our survival, emotional, and spiritual needs.

Gratitude is an invitation to God to enter our lives and fill our existence with blessing. Maintaining a state of gratitude allows us to keep the signal of the divine transmission ever clear in our hearts.

With gratitude, we learn to embody freedom. Stuck in the cage of the ego, a sense of entitlement develops. We become selfish and that creates desire. From this sense of nonfulfillment emptiness arises in the heart. Being in service to others is one of the best possible means to shift perspective. When we shift focus from ourselves and our own unhappiness to doing for another, we begin to realize our purpose in life. Because we are all one being, when we serve others, we serve ourselves. We become grateful for the little things and develop gratitude for all things.

When you are feeling down and disconnected, go do something for someone else. It doesn't matter what. It could be helping someone with a task at work, lending an ear to one who is suffering, or doing something nice for a random person. It does not matter what you are doing, but that you are doing it for someone else. Do this service selflessly without expecting anything in return. Detach from the fruits of your labor. You become grateful in the unbound sense of freedom that develops as you realize your purpose. This reminds me of St Francis' prayer where he asked God to help him, "not so much seek to be consoled as to console, to be understood as to understand, to be loved as to love, for it is in giving we receive, in pardoning we are pardoned, in dying to the self we are born to eternal life". Shifting focus from the self to another is a perfect example of the expression of gratitude. Since we are all connected, doing service for another is doing service for ourselves.

Understanding the frequency of gratitude helps to maintain the highest vibration in the heart. Gratitude and discontentment are opposites on the energetic scale of the heart. They cannot manifest simultaneously in our lives. We either are in a state of gratitude or discontent. We do not experience both at the same time. Selfishness shifts our focus toward discontentment. Selfishness creates attachments and, "attachment breeds desire" as the Bhagavad Gita states. This desire gets us stuck in the unhappiness of wanting what we do not have. We become discontent with this state of fulfillment and if you stay here long enough you become hopelessly overwhelmed.

Humility gives us the ability to transform our energy. Humility gives us the ability to see we are only one piece in a much larger puzzle. Coming to this understanding we can serve others. There is great satisfaction in selfless service because we are manifesting our purpose. We develop gratitude in our lives and because of this gratitude we begin seeing blessings that encompass our lives like rain covers the sky. When we stop being self-centered, instead we create in ourselves a center of service for the world!

Dealing with difficult or challenging people is an opportunity for spiritual development. We get a chance to use the other person as a mirror and realize the aspects of ourselves we are not satisfied with and change them. We should be grateful for challenging people in our lives because without them how could we ever grow? Choose to see the divine spark in these people. It may be extraordinarily difficult, but imagine what they would look like if they were functioning from the highest capacity of their heart. Then only will you understand how to help them get there. At first, serving others may be through energetic meditation, by mentally projecting your perception of their higher self. Eventually, you will be able to assist them with some type of physical guidance. Everyone has an inner light. Your responsibility as a spiritual aspirant is to bring that light out in everyone you with whom you come into contact.

Gandhi gave us an idea that has really helped me to befriend those who trouble me. "Truth resides in every human heart, and one has to search for it there and be guided by truth as one sees it. But no one has a right to coerce others to act according to his own view of the truth"

We all maintain our own understanding of truth. When we come to appreciate the truths of others (especially our opponents) we come to befriend and ascend all barriers. Disagreements fade away as we learn to radiate peace amongst each other. Gandhi was grateful for his opponents as they served as the medium for catalyzing his spiritual development. He amazingly cultivated a gratitude for his imprisonment. The jail he was confined in was known as the Yerdava Prison. He referred to it as the Yerdava Temple. When you maintain a constant connection with God, everyplace you are becomes sacred, even a jail! Living in love gives you the ability to find gratitude in every moment.

Gratitude is the absolute cure for depression. When a person feels down in the dumps, he or she has lost appreciation for even the little things in life. When they reconnect with a sense of gratitude, their depression goes away instantly. Whatever the reason behind the depression, being thankful for our blessings cures the cause of the malady. One practice I have found to kindle a sense of appreciation is to make a list of 10 things I am grateful for. It is a very powerful meditation. Try it the next time you feel depressed, unhappy, or are struggling emotionally with a challenge. You will reconnect to a place of appreciation and reinvigorate your life with the transformative energy of gratitude.

Compassion

My teacher Tim Miller leads my favorite yoga retreat annually in Mt. Shasta, California. It is an amazing retreat. Students practice pranayama (deep breathing) and asana (yoga postures) with Tim every morning, followed by hikes, and discourses on yoga in the evening. For me, it is the most blissful time of year. When I get home from the retreat, I often find myself coming down from an emotional peak. Sometime I have felt sad or even depressed returning to the concrete jungle we know as our civilization.

I asked Tim, "How do I maintain that feeling of bliss I connect with at the retreat all year round?" Expecting some lengthy discourse or a quote from the Yoga Sutras, Tim turned to me and laughingly said, "Be compassionate to yourself and others". His simple answer blew me away. Pearls of wisdom from the Guru.

This began my journey toward understanding and ultimately living with self-compassion. But first what is compassion? It is beyond love. Most people love expecting something in return. *Compassion is love in action*. Love without expecting anything in return. Real love is what the soul needs instead of what the ego wants. Compassion is a celestial quality. When we are honest with ourselves, we realize the struggles we are facing in life may not be exactly what we want but they are exactly what we need to take the next evolutionary step toward developing spiritual understanding. The divine order of the universe does not make mistakes. When you understand this truth, you have reason to find gratitude for even the greatest challenges in life. When you face life's obstacles with gratitude your heart remains open allowing you to tap into the unlimited power of devotion! With devotion, you will find the ability to move mountains.

Being compassionate to yourself requires a great deal of honesty. It is easy to fall prey to the desire of the ego instead of the universal desire. The ego is very tricky and sinister.

Maintaining your sadhana, or daily spiritual practice, is the most compassionate thing you can do for yourself. You may not always want to get up early for yoga or meditation practice, but those are the days you tend to have the biggest breakthroughs and realizations. Your sadhana gives you the insight to know what you need to live your purpose.

Compassion does not necessarily mean instant gratification. Take, for instance, your physical yoga practice. You may induce moments of discomfort or suffering to advance physically, emotionally, and spiritually. We do not practice because it always feels good. We practice because it makes us more able to handle life outside of the context of the yoga studio or meditation center. Like brushing your teeth every morning, we practice daily because it maintains our physical, mental, and spiritual hygiene.

It is easy to be kind to others when they are kind to us. It is saintly to be kind to those who are mean to us. This is true compassion. Jesus Christ is one of the best examples of living compassion. When he was dying on the cross, suffering greatly at the hands of his captors, he asked God to, "Forgive them Father for they know not what they do". People are often unkind because of ignorance. Listening to the intuition gained from meditation guides you on the path of compassion. In the face of ignorance, your compassionate may inspire transformation and awareness in others.

Being compassionate to others gives you an opportunity to evaluate the big picture in your own life and overcome personal struggles. Once I got into a horrible argument with my roommate. It was so bad; the only option left was for me to move out of the house immediately. At first, I was very upset at him and felt insecure and angry. I sat in meditation about this predicament and surprisingly connected with feelings of gratitude and compassion toward my friend.

Meditation allowed me to heighten my vibration, disassociate with my emotions and come to a place of humility.

I realized that we were not compatible living together. Finding a different living situation was in both of our best interests. As uncomfortable as the argument was and moving promised to be, I was grateful I would no longer be in the incompatible living arrangement and would afford myself a better opportunity for spiritual development. I could be compassionate and stop harboring negative feelings and could wish only the best for my friend. This was not easy at first because I felt I had been wronged, but when I allowed myself to experience these feelings, I discovered another dimension of freedom. Being mad at my friend held me back, not him. The Buddha taught, "Anger is like grabbing a hot coal to throw at someone else and expecting them to get burned."

Attachment to my residence distorted my perception of reality. Being compassionate to myself allowed me to sit, meditate and catalyze several deeper realizations. Compassion brings light like a candle to a dark room. Search your own life for ways to be more compassionate to yourself and others.

Next I will share a powerful meditation with you that charges each chakra with the mighty power of gratitude. Each chakra has both positive and negative characteristics associated with its manifestation. This meditation guides you to access the more beneficial element of each chakra as you align and harmonize each energy center with gratitude.

Gratitude Meditation

Begin focusing on your breathing as you connect to a centered space of harmony within. Spend a few minutes paying attention to the quality of your inhales and exhales.

When you are ready, begin inhaling and exhaling the color red through the top of the head. Allow yourself to feel gratitude toward any aspect in your life you associate with survival. It could be food, your home, clothing, your job, anything. Now let go of the survival element and simply sit with the feeling of gratitude itself.

Shifting to the second chakra inhale and exhale the color orange through the top of the head. Think of an experience of pleasure you are grateful for. Maybe the taste of your favorite food, a wonderful vacation, intercourse with your partner. It could be any pleasurable experience. Now let go of the experience and sit with the feeling of gratitude for the experience.

Onto the third chakra. Breath in and out the color yellow. Think of an empowering experience where you made a difference in the world. Examples include helping your children, making an impact at work, helping the homeless or elderly. Now sit with the feeling of gratitude for that experience itself.

In the fourth chakra breath in and out the color green. Allow yourself to experience gratitude for a person who has inspired or assisted you in your life. It could be a teacher, coworker, family member or anyone else who comes to mind. Now let go of the specific person and simply sit with the feeling of gratitude.

For the fifth chakra breath in and out the color blue. Think of an experience in which you manifested the brilliance of your creativity. Feel an appreciation for that experience. Now let go of the circumstances and just sit with the feeling of gratitude.

Breath in and out the color indigo for the sixth chakra. Think of a time when you listened to your intuition and were led to

> making an important decision. Now let go of the circumstance and sit with the feeling of gratitude for the experience itself.
>
> Breath in and out the color violet for the crown chakra. Remember a time when you experienced peace or tranquility at an unprecedented level. Feel grateful for this experience. Now allow let go of the experience and just sit with the feeling.
>
> Allow gratitude to infuse through every atom of your body. Each beat of the heart pumps gratitude through your blood. Lose yourself in the magnificence of gratitude.
>
> Take a few natural breaths and when you are ready slowly open your eyes.

Each time you practice this meditation, you will likely remember different experiences for each chakra. This is a good thing because ultimately, we are not working toward remembering specific experiences, rather cultivating a sense of gratitude for all creation. Accumulating gratitude harmonizes your essence with the essence of the universe. Being grateful demonstrates to the universe that you have learned and internalized your current lessons and are ready for more. Gratitude serves as a prerequisite and the proof that more is coming in your life.

Get deep into the practice of appreciation. Allow yourself to feel grateful for everything in your life. Even obstacles hide great opportunities, so learn to appreciate your challenges because those difficulties inspire your evolution and guide you toward your destiny and purpose. Gratitude acts as the key to the door of the heart. Keep that door wide open by vigilantly maintaining gratitude in all your thoughts, beliefs, and actions.

Chapter 4: Living in Harmony

"The wise live without injuring nature as the bee drinks nectar without harming the flower."
-The Buddha

Modern culture is in a state of artificial intelligence. By artificial intelligence, I do not mean we have created a computer with the technology to replicate human thought. I am using this term to describe society's current state of psychological conditioning. We have collectively given away our intelligence, our ability to discern, to the discretion of the mass media. We have surrendered our intelligence to an artificial system created by greed. This system hypnotizes us through the manipulation of our own desires. Thomas Jefferson wrote a treatise about how the modern system of currency is a form of disguised slavery. He was describing how people's thoughts and actions could be controlled by manipulating their desires. There is a way out of this material bondage; a way back to our birthright of freedom.

We must attune ourselves with the divine frequency that created and powers all life. This divine current is not only in all of us but it connects each of us to everyone, everything, and even to the planet itself. Heightening awareness of our cultural conditioning begins the process of de-hypnotization, the first step in realizing our true identity. There is a difference between knowing and realizing. Knowing is having the information. Realizing is embodying the truth and doing something about it. We all know we have given up our power to materialism, but most of us are not willing to do anything about it. Meditation brings us to a realization that empowers us to make transformational changes in ourselves and the world around us. Through meditation we learn to control the urges of our senses.

Desire hides the knowledge of our inner truth. With meditation, we gain the strength to turn awareness inside which gives us the ability to fight selfishness. Realizing the interconnectedness of all life is the ability to orient yourself toward the will of the divine.

Living in harmony with the world happens because of deconditioning. You begin to make decisions based on a higher consciousness, a deeper understanding. Learning how to use money is a tricky game. Money itself is not bad. Money is the physical manifestation of prana, our divine energy. Greed and selfishness created by the desire for more money than needed is the evil that plagues society today. But money itself essentially is neither good nor bad. How we make and use money determines the level of harmony we experience. Attachment to money is not a good thing. Realizing the nature of money and using it for a just means is understanding **and** living a universal truth.

Before becoming a yoga asana instructor, I worked as a real estate agent during one of the worst downward trends in the history of our nation's economy. People were losing their homes right and left because of shady practices of real estate agents, loans agents, and, most of all, the big banking industry.

After completing my yoga teachers training, I underwent a tremendous awakening in my life. I realized the preciousness and the impermanence of our lives. How we chose to spend our time is vitally important. I was working on a deal where I stood to profit by helping a bank evict a family of eight and moving a family of three into the home. After closing the deal, I took the money I made and opened a yoga studio leaving the practice of real estate for good. The ethics gained from heightening my consciousness would only allow me to give back to the world. We are faced with choices every day that determine the level of harmony we personally choose to live in. The means in which you work, make money, and spend your money should be ethical and altruistic. To live in harmony, what you do must be of benefit to the greater society. Harming

others for profit is unharmonious and will only create negative karma in your life.

The *universal law of fair trade exists* to help us realize our purpose. The law works similarly to the concept of karma. When you serve someone else you will be rewarded through the universal order one way or another. You do not have to work solely for money. You work because your purpose is to help others along in their own personal journey of evolution. We do not have to work just to make money. When you serve others, you know you are serving a purpose and doing the right thing with your time and energy. Your purpose is to serve not to earn capitol but you will be rewarded. Remember Einstein's theory of relativity states energy can neither be created nor destroyed only transformed. When you work for others your energy will be transformed to something else you can utilize.

Working strictly for money means working to fulfill one's own selfish desires. Work from your heart doing what you love to do and you will be compensated one way or another. But remember to stay in that abode of love, operate in service to the divine and your fellow human being. This way you are serving the divine will, not your own ego.

How you spend the money you make is very important to staying in harmony. Often when you pay more for the same goods or services you are getting more. Take for instance grocery shopping. You may be able to buy goods for less money shopping at a large corporation like Wal-Mart instead of a store like Whole Foods. Wal-Mart treats their employees very poorly, making them work only part-time with no benefits or possibility of promotions. Wal-Mart also purchases goods from Third World nations at the lowest price possible, even utilizing child labor.

Whole Foods gives its employees benefits, opportunities for advancement and full-time hours. Not to mention Whole Foods maintains values that place a high priority on ethically sustaining the environment (for example selling fish that is sustainably farmed). The same item may be 25 percent less at Wal-Mart but you are receiving 100 percent more at Whole Foods for your purchase. This is just one example of spending your money more consciously.

As you heighten your consciousness, you realize more ways to benefit the world by spending the same money with greater awareness. You may choose to do you banking at an establishment that supports the local community or the environment. Maybe you do online research about how specific clothing companies use eco-friendly dyes. At my yoga studio, we sold clothes that were made by a company named "Prana". Prana purchased clean air energy credits for every vendor who sold their apparel. Just by carrying their clothes made the studio a clean energy establishment. Another example is paying a little more for cleaning products (soaps, bathroom cleaner, detergents, etc.) that do not test on animals and are more environmentally friendly.

These small changes are all results of raising your awareness and making the conscious decision to live at a greater level of harmony with the environment. The Native American mystic Wolf Song of the Abenaki tribe imparts tremendous wisdom in his statement about playing our part in the circle of life:

To honor and respect means to think of the land and the water and plants and animals who live here as having a right equal to our own to be here. We are not the supreme and all-knowing beings, living at the top of the pinnacle of evolution, but in fact we are members of the sacred hoop of life, along with the trees and rocks, the coyotes and the eagles and fish and toads, that each fulfills its purpose. They each perform their given task in the sacred hoop, and we have one too.

Allow yourself to live a little more deeply. It is OK to sing. It is good to dance (even if you are not good at it). Ancient cultures have been singing and dancing since the advent of time. It is part of being human. We get so caught up in our image that it becomes customary to close off huge aspects of our authentic selves. It is not about how you look; it's about how you feel. Maya Angelou said it best: "People don't remember you by what you said. People don't remember you by what you did. People remember you by how you make them feel."

Search in the depths of your heart for how deeply you can love. The famous Saint Francis' prayer for peace, states "not so much to be loved as to love." How much can you love until you lose yourself in love? God is love and you are love. Awakening to this reality is connecting to the greatest truth in the world. When you begin the journey down this rabbit hole, you follow the path of infinite, unbound, immortal bliss. In finding this union with the divine you realize that you yourself are and always have been divine. Now let your divinity permeate from the inside out in harmony with the universe.

Next, we will go over a meditation practice designed to help you connect to the divine presence of nature all around you. I can recall few experiences as powerful as realizing the beauty and exquisiteness of nature permeating through my being. Heaven and hell do not exist after our departure from the physical realm. Rather these states are meant to describe the quality of existence we have created with our own thought process. This meditation helps me reconnect to reality and correct my thinking. As I reap, I sow. What I believe, I create. I choose to be the intermediary, the living connection between heaven and earth in my own personal reality. Make the conscious decision to manifest the divine in every aspect of your life.

> **Heaven and Earth Meditation**
>
> Begin to connect and center yourself with your breathing. Take three deep breaths. Spend as long as you need coming to a state of inner balance by concentrating on your breath.
>
> Take a long inhale breathing into the center of your chest. As you exhale, imagine roots growing out of the bottom of your feet and diving into the earth beneath you. As you inhale, breathe in the energy and nourishment provided to you by mother earth. Exhale and grow your roots deeper into the planet. Again, inhale the enriching life energy of nature. Spend a few minutes connecting to the world.
>
> When you are ready, inhale into the center of your chest. As you exhale imagine a tree sprouting out of the top of your head and reaching toward the heavens. Inhale and breathe in the divine light from the spiritual realm. Exhale and watch as your tree climbs higher into the heavens. Inhale in the spirit and exhale into your growing tree of life. Spend as long as you like here.
>
> Now take an inhale to into the center of your chest. As you exhale, breathe out through your roots and through the trunk, branches, and leaves of your tree. Breathe in all of nature's nourishment to your core. Breath out as you deepen your earthly and celestial connections. Spend as long as you like here.
>
> When you are ready, come back to the natural rhythm of your breath. Take three more deep breaths and slowly begin to open your eyes.

    One of the most beautiful realizations a person can come to in meditation is that we can connect to a deeper reality at any time and place regardless of the circumstances. The most effective way to transform the world around us is to transform the word inside. This ability is innate. All you must do is devote the time and energy to maintain the meditation practice that is most appropriate for you. There are an infinite number of types of meditation. Experiment with several different forms. When you find that method that is most appropriate for you, stick to it. Devote yourself to the practice. Embrace it. Throw yourself into it until you have clearly seen the light and discover the truth. As Christ said, "The kingdom of heaven is within you". All you have to do is seek and you will find it.

The Waterfall

A young man sat gazing into a waterfall. He was watching other boys jump from the waterfall into the lake below. It looked like a great deal of fun but the young man accepted his fate, that he would not be able to enjoy the experience. The young man was born crippled and could not walk. He watched the waterfall empty into the lake from a wheelchair.

Suddenly and seemingly out of nowhere, Lord Krishna appeared to the boy. Krishna asked him, "Why aren't you jumping into the lake like all the other boys?" The young man replied, "I cannot walk, how am I supposed to climb to the top of the waterfall and jump off?" Krishna told him, "Do not worry, I will carry you."

Reluctantly, with a powerful underlying current of excitement, the young man agreed. With his arms wrapped around Krishna's neck, the pair ascended the cliff face. At the top, they could see the lake and it looked like a very long fall. Fear began to set in with the boy. He told Krishna, "I will not be able to jump, I can't even stand on my own." Krishna replied, "Don't worry, we will jump together." So together, arm in arm, Krishna and the boy jumped from the top of the waterfall into the lake. The fall was amazing, weightless and exhilarating. The young man had never felt anything like it before. They submerged in the lake together, but only the boy came up for air. Krishna was nowhere to be seen. The boy swam to the edge of the lake where he walked out on his own two feet. It was a miracle! From then on the boy could walk.

News of the miracle spread throughout the land. The lake became a sacred place. Others who made pilgrimages to the lake and experienced miracles merely by entering its waters. One man was healed of cancer. Another woman regained the ability to see. So, on and so forth many miracles took place there. The legend of the lake grew and grew. Hundreds and eventually thousands began to make the pilgrimage daily. Vendors started putting up tents on the shores of the lake. First, they started selling food. Then vendors started selling souvenirs and trinkets. One man started bottling water from the lake and selling it. Another showed up and started selling a book. Little by little the lake became a place for much commerce. And one day, people stopped experiencing miracles at the lake. It was no longer a sacred, revered place. The lake lost its power. The people lost the ability to use its power.

How in our world have we lost the ability to see the sacredness in all things? We allow capitalism, industry, commerce, and materialism to cloud our perception of spirituality. You see, God is always there, every moment is sacred, but do we choose to perceive life in such a way? Enlightenment is the ability to see the interconnectedness in all things. Greed, desire, and attachment keep us disconnected from the whole. With humility, we can rediscover that place inside ourselves. The place is one yearning for connection with the ethereal. By realigning our desire and intentions with our higher energy centers (love, creativity, intuition, and spirituality), it is possible to rediscover the true self. The seer in all things is God. God is the seer of all things through you. When you find your center and purge clean every layer of self from the inside out you will know yourself and the world will see you clearly.

Chapter 5: Lighting Your Fire

To double your net worth, double your self-worth. Because you will never exceed the height of your self-image.

-Robin Sharma

Boredom to Inspiration

Boredom and inspiration are the same energy moving in opposite directions. What separates the two is a sense of purpose. When I am bored, I find myself lacking direction, not connecting with my purpose. Boredom is quite debilitating. When you tell yourself you are bored, you become discontent at being in the moment, being in your own skin. This state must change for you to begin moving forward on your spiritual journey and experience contentment.

To switch the direction of the energy you must connect to a sense of purpose. Meditation is a powerful tool to turn the tide. When a person is stressed his or her mind does not function at full capacity. Meditation helps you to relax and improve your brain function. Ideas start to flow through you. You can more effectively identify what is important to you.

Ask yourself, what is the most important change needed in the world today? Maybe the environment, a political issue, helping the sick, orphaned, or homeless. Whatever matter your heart gravitates toward most strongly is your purpose. What can you do to manifest the changes you see necessary? Through meditation you can identify and create action steps to realize your purpose. With this purpose, you transform boredom to inspiration. Living your purpose is taking action to manifest the change you understand is most required in the world. The more action you take the more inspired you become.

For me, when I am not writing, teaching, or helping others in some way, I quickly become bored and frustrated with life. I start to think, "what is the point?" and when this thinking increases, I find myself moving toward depression. When I notice myself running this cycle, the first thing I do is cut straight through to reality by sitting down and meditating. By utilizing this practice, I reconnect to my purpose. I remember what I am here for. To inspire others, I have to remain inspired myself. And motivation is a symbiotic relationship because the best way for me to find inspiration is to inspire others.

The next step is almost always to sit down and write. I write whatever is in my mind and heart regardless if it seems to correlate with my current work (and without realizing it, it almost always does). When I write something powerful that touches others, I become inspired. By maintaining this practice constantly, my levels of inspiration and impact on the world around me remain high. By living my purpose, I live life inspired and that is the best way to assist in manifesting the changes I see necessary in the world.

Inspiration

I have been asked, "Why do you spend so much time and energy helping people"? I believe that people can evolve, that people can change. Even if you do not believe in yourself, I believe in you and your greatness. I believe in you so much that one day it might even inspire you to believe in yourself.

In biology, we examine the life of a cell. A cell is either dying or thriving. It is either helping to create more cells or it is on its way out. People are the same in the sense we are either living a mediocre life or we are living a world-class existence. You are either massively underperforming or you are thriving and realizing your dreams. There is no idle path in life. Average is mediocre. The light switch is either on or off. The goal is to thrive, to live in enlightenment, to hit the target in this lifetime.

When you are living an average life, there is lots of competition. It is a dog eat dog world. You are in the back of the pack just fighting for you spot to be in the rat race. When you are living a world-class life, you are a front-runner, an innovator in your field. Being world class eliminates competition. When you are in the front of the pack, there are few if any competitors who can keep pace with you. When you are working to realize your purpose, the universe will do everything it can to make your dreams a reality. The impossible becomes reality. No one dreams small. Dream big, go after your heart's desire no matter how unrealistic your dreams may seem now. Your purpose is to realize your dream. So, going after that dream is exactly what you need to be doing. There are many trails to get to the top of a mountain. Realizing your purpose may not materialize the exact way you originally plan, but it will not materialize at all unless you fight for it like a drowning man fights for air.

Some people may call you crazy for chasing after your dreams, but know there is a big difference between crazy and eccentric. Someone who is crazy is not grounded in reality, is not following their heart, and is not channeling the divine. Needless to say, there are a lot of crazy people out there.

When you are eccentric, you will likely appear crazy to crazy people. The eccentric realizes his dreams by staying grounded while following his heart and creating a divine vision for reality. It may seem crazy to dream big. Living your vision makes the impossible a reality. When you start to believe, you start to achieve.

An unlikely example for a book about spirituality is Mike Tyson. He probably became one of the greatest fighters who ever lived - once he believed in himself. He learned to box in prison. From the lowest place you can fall to in our culture, he realized his dream and became the most dominant boxer of his time. How did he reach such remarkable heights from such insurmountable depths?

Someone believed in him. A man used to go in to the juvenile detention facility where Tyson was imprisoned. His name was Cus Dimato. He was hard on Tyson, but through adversity Tyson's skill began to flourish. Dimato saw Tyson's potential and nourished it. Dimato moved Tyson into his own home as soon as he left jail. No one had ever believed in Tyson before, including himself. Every day while Dimato trained Tyson he told the young boxer, "You're gonna be champion of the world one day". Tyson thought the old man was crazy. He did not know about being eccentric. Dimato kept telling his fighter he would be a world champion every day. So much so that eventually Tyson began to believe that he would be a world champion one day. Tyson began to create this belief in himself. Not long after, Tyson won a gold medal in the Olympics with the fastest knock out in history. Not long after that, Tyson won the World Boxing Organization's world title again with the fastest knock out in history (13 seconds)!

Dimato's passing sent Tyson's life into a tailspin. Tyson stopped believing in himself, stopped living his purpose and began to lose fights he should have won or should never even taken in the first place. Tyson made the shift from eccentric to crazy.

Once you've found that belief in yourself, you must keep doing things to nourish your vision daily. You must stay inspired. What got you inspired in the first place? Was it a specific person? Seek our more people like that. Surround yourself with inspiring people who feed your belief in yourself. The people you keep around drastically affect your positivity level. Be very discerning about who you let in your inner circle. Notice if an individual inspires you or needs to be inspired by you. Do the practices of yoga and meditation help you to stay grounded and inspired while working toward your dream? They absolutely do (believe it or not Tyson used to practice yoga during his meteoric rise).

Spiritual practices are designed to ground you while you traverse your path. Maintain some type of daily spiritual practice. Especially when life seem the busiest, maintain a consistent spiritual practice. This is how you will stay grounded, connected to the heart, and able to realize each step of your vision. And lastly remember inspiration is infectious. When you share your inspiration with others, you in turn renew your inspirational energy. Then the other person shares it with someone else. When you share inspiration, you pay it forward truly making the world a better place. Do the things that keep your fire lit. Pay attention to when that fire starts to wane so you can cultivate more inspiration.

Intrinsic vs. Extrinsic Motivation

In the organizational behavior model, motivation is considered either intrinsic or extrinsic. A good rule of thumb to understand the difference is to look at the prefix of the words. Intrinsic (in) implies internal. Extrinsic (ex) refers to external. Understanding types of motivation helps us to cultivate a passion for life and maintain high levels of motivation.

Extrinsic motivation tends to be short-term factors that encourage us to strive for physical or material rewards. An example would be going to work every day to earn a paycheck on Friday. The paycheck is the motivating force that encourages us to get up, go to work every day and bring home the money. A weekly paycheck is a form of short-term motivation. If it were not for that weekly paycheck, you would probably not go to work. There is nothing wrong with that. It is important to identify the type and source of motivation to improve the quality of work and increase the duration of inspiration.

Intrinsic motivation refers to long-term factors that encourage us to thrive in working for internal factors such as spirituality values, realizing your purpose, improving a sense of well-being. An example would be working in the field of health care because you believe in the importance of serving others and improving the quality of life for all. You are not working toward a short-term goal. Rather you are striving for a broader, long-term goal of improving the quality of life for all.

Extrinsic motivation has a temporary, short-term effect. Intrinsic motivation has a long-term effect. Extrinsic is not as effective as intrinsic motivation in the overall scheme of things. Extrinsic motivation is good but it is limited by time and results. Intrinsic motivation is better because it is unlimited by time and has boundless results.

Examining what motivates us in life improves the quality and duration of our effort. Find ways to transform extrinsic to intrinsic motivation in your life and have a greater more positive influence on the world. Use extrinsic motivating factors to get the ball rolling. Transform extrinsic to intrinsic motivators to keep the ball rolling and create a snowball effect of success.

I propose another element to the motivational model of organizational behavior. There is another echelon of motivation that encourages our development by the humblest means: altruistic motivation. Altruism is defined as "with regard for or devotion to the well-being of others". Altruistic motivation is the inspiration to action for the welfare of those outside the self. There is nothing that makes life more fulfilling that the art of living selflessly. The ultimate degree of motivation is that which impels us to action for the benefit of the greater good. Time goes by more quickly, the universe seems to always operate in your favor, and you will without a doubt be living on purpose.

Altruistic motivation has neither a short or long-term effect but a permanent everlasting benefit to its adherent and the world around him or her. Practice altruistic motivation through selfless service regardless of more apparent extrinsic and even intrinsic motivational factors and your compensation will seem limitless.

Honestly identify which level of motivation impels you most regularly in life be it extrinsic, intrinsic, or altruistic. Ultimately the type of motivation that moves an individual determines the effects of their thoughts and actions on themselves and others. Your predominant type of motivation determines your reality. Increase the quality of your impact by evolving the space from where you derive motivation.

Deficiency vs. Growth Motivation

In the early 1940s and '50s Abraham Maslow, a prominent psychologist developed of a new theory about motivation. Maslow devoted a great deal of time to studying individuals he described as self-actualizers with the hope of finding a common link between such individuals. Once identifying these traits, he could work at cultivating these qualities in others and assist them toward their own selfactualization. By self-actualizers, Maslow was referring to highly successful people. They could quite possibly be referred to as self-realized or enlightened. Whatever you choose to call them, these individuals possess some highly effective traits and habits that enabled them to realize their purpose.

Some traits of self-actualizers are: seeing problems as challenges and situations requiring solutions; having the need for privacy or alone time; socially compassionate, comfortable with themselves; excited even in the ordinary tasks of life; few close friends instead of a multitude of shallow relationships; democratic and fair; unsusceptible to social pressures; rely on their own experiences instead of cultural opinions and views, accepting others as they are and not try to change people, spontaneous, creative, seeking peak experiences that leave long term impressions, among many other traits. Maslow created a hierarchy of needs often displayed as a pyramid. The first level of the pyramid has biological and physiological needs: air, food, drink, shelter, sex, sleep etc. Second are safety needs: protection from elements, security, order, law, limits, and stability. Third are love needs: work group, family, affection, and relationships. Fourth are esteem needs: self-esteem, achievement, mastery, independence, status, dominance, prestige, and managerial responsibility. The fifth level of the pyramid is the peak, self-actualization needs: realizing personal potential, self-fulfillment, seeking personal growth, and peak experiences.

  Maslow described two types of motivation: deficiency motivation and growth motivation. The four lowest steps of the model of hierarchy are deficiency motivated. The fifth step of the pyramid represents growth motivation. The vast majority of people in our modern culture can identify with deficiency motivation. Most focus on what lacks in their lives. The needs, wants, and desires drive their every thought and action. Deficiency motivation is inspiration derived from assessing the factors that are missing or lacking in one's life and planning a course of action to fulfill those deficiencies. "I need a better car so I am going to work as hard as I can until I save enough money to afford one", "I need to lose weight so I am going to diet until I attain my weight loss goal," and, "I want to improve my reputation, so I am going to start wearing expensive clothes to improve my appearance" are all examples of deficiency motivation and the thinking they disseminate.

  The great conundrum with deficiency motivation is that it is a total set up for failure in attaining the goal of happiness. When creating and striving toward a desire for more, the result is the creation of another desire for more. This is an endlessly perpetual cycle. You set a goal to make one million dollars.

When you achieve the goal, you have bought an expensive home and car, have high payments and now need two million dollars. By the time you reach that goal, your needs will have doubled. The disease becomes a never-ending continuum. You will always be struggling for more and never and never arrive at a destination of peace. This is how some of the wealthiest people experience the greatest levels of discontent. Happiness will never be attainable. When you habitually train yourself to incessantly need more. To find what is lacking becomes the precedent, focusing on what you do not have becomes the goal. Our thoughts create the reality we experience. Through deficiency motivation we create a reality of unending dissatisfaction.

I hope you have had enough of this deficiency motivation because I have had enough writing about it. Let's shift gears to the most important trait of self-actualizers, growth motivation. This type of mindset is dramatically different from the ladder. An individual established in growth motivation chooses to focus on his or her innate qualities that will always enable success. This though process would sound of the tune, "I possess the mental capability to graduate college", "My focus and determination will enable me to finish this marathon", and "connecting to the infinite inner space within makes meditation not only possible but entirely enjoyable". Growth motivation shifts your focus from what you do not have to what you have always had and will always have. You have more power than you have given yourself credit for. To realize this capability, begin by creating a space in your mind to access it. Access comes from focusing on what you innately have instead of what you incessantly want. With this type of thinking, dreams become not only a possibility but an actuality. The lacks fade away into the oblivion of their innate illusion. When you focus on what you have instead of what you desire, living your purpose becomes your course. All previous desires are par for the course yet you earn more than you have ever dreamed.

For the purpose of better understanding the difference between deficiency and growth motivation, imagine a tree. Let's say that rate at which this tree grows is determined by its quality of motivation. If the tree was deficiency motivated, it would focus on everything it lacks. The tree would be stressed by periods of little or no water, poor soil, changing temperatures, and the shortage of sunlight on cloudy days. This tree would likely fair miserably with the common conditions experienced by nearly all trees.

Luckily for trees, nature is growth motivated. The tree empowered by growth motivation focuses on what it does have. It is grateful for the water it does have and stores extra water for times of drought. Trees stretch out their roots deep into the soil to access the abundance of nutrients, minerals, and hydration they are innately provided by nature. Trees utilize the process of photosynthesis enabling them to serve all life, humans and animals, by converting carbon dioxide into the oxygen we depend on for survival. Being growth motivated allows trees to play their role in the circle of life and in turn they experience the ever-present abundance of the planet.

Think of the cactus found in a desert. These plants experience the harshest of earth's weather conditions yet continue to thrive. Instead of struggling from a lack of water, the cactus focus on conserving and efficiently utilizing the water they do have. Cacti even serve the birds and bees by providing them with flowers for their nourishment. In turn, birds and bees pollinate cacti so they can flower and flourish.

Redwoods are another great example. You would think the phenomenon of forest fires would decimate an ancient tree like the redwood. This is not the case, because redwoods are growth motivated. Forest fires increase the number of redwoods because the forest floor is opened for younger plant life to harvest sunlight only made available by the absence of the tallest trees. The charred remains of the burnt trees replenish the soil with nitrogen creating the perfect habitat for the younger trees to thrive. Only by focusing on what they have instead of what they do not have, members of the plant kingdom have been able to flourish throughout the eons.

People can follow the example of how to manifest the bounty so ever abundant in nature by utilizing their innate tendencies and qualities instead of worrying about challenges and obstacles that exist only to be overcome. Obstacles are opportunities for growth. It is ever important to use them this way.

Alignment

Alignment is so precious. Being a yoga instructor, it is easy to see when students are in or out of alignment. When we are out of alignment, everything hurts and growth is impossible. In alignment, the practice seems to flow effortlessly and growth is constant. To gain alignment when it is lacking requires a shift in perspective, and increase in humility and honesty. Such an adjustment can come from the instructor or the practitioner herself. With this newfound alignment, the practice becomes enjoyable and much more beneficial.

This principle of alignment is applicable both on and off the yoga mat. In life, alignment is crucial. When we are living out of alignment with our core values, we make mistakes we would not have otherwise and cause much suffering in our own and others' lives. To regain alignment in life, requires a shift in perception. The cause of misalignment with our values is the ego. When we become honest with ourselves, we can realign our life with our values and reconnect with our own true vibrant self. Meditation and yoga practice, teachers, friends, and family are all excellent guides to help us shift our perspective back to reality. Physical alignment translates to clarity of mind, which transforms to a connection with the heart.

Intention

"Our life is shaped by our mind for we become what we think"
-Buddha

Intention is a very important principle for those adhering to the spiritual path. The evolutionary journey has trained the brain to seek stimulation as a means for survival for protection and enjoyment. By setting a clear intention, it becomes possible to maintain focus and to embark on the course to experience greater peace and tranquility.

Before evolving to its modern state, humankind still lived in the wild. Man had a closer connection to his animal roots and had not yet achieved the prevailing title of apex predator. We were still very vulnerable to being attacked and harmed by wild animals on a regular basis. Man lived in huntergatherer groups of 150 or fewer people. The invention of farming created the means to form larger groups and eventually cities.

Our brain evolved to protect us from the potential of being harmed by developing systems to keep attention sharp and help us to stay safe. The brain manages three thought processes: holding onto mental information; changing the focus of attention; and seeking a point of stimulation. Thousands of years ago in the wild, the brain had to hold onto information of potential risk factors, like an animal moving in the bushes. Next the brain needed to update its focus point either from external or internal factors, such as an animal appearing or recalling ancestral water source. And lastly the brain learned to seek further stimulation to continue the hunt for food or resources.

Having to juggle these three elements of attention can make it seem impossible to focus. Understanding how our cerebral anatomy has developed can help us arrive at a method to focusing the three-ringed circus of the monkey mind. When you try to hold a point of focus in the brain like meditating or completing a project at work, the mind forms a kind of gate shutting out all other thoughts and distractions. Inside this gate the happiness-infusing neurochemical dopamine is produced, keeping the entryway closed and all distractions out. When you start to experience boredom, the stimulation subsides, dopamine ceases to flow and the gate opens shifting our attention elsewhere. Inversely a rapid spike in dopamine can be caused by a pertinent external factor like the phone ringing, someone knocking on the door or a pretty girl walking by which will avert attention. The process was designed by evolution to keep us safe from potential predators and continue acquiring resources. The next step in our spiritual evolution will require us to evolve the mind by setting an intention as a means of maintaining focus in meditation and daily life.

Knowing the mind has an innate tendency to fluctuate makes it even more important to set a concrete positive intention before beginning any task such as working or meditation. When we form a positive intention, the continuous stream of dopamine is strengthened in our mind giving us a greater ability to maintain focus. As you practice this method you become more efficient and eventually you will develop a laser beam of focus.

Before you begin a task or start the day, reaffirm to yourself that this task is going to be enjoyable or that today is going to be a great day. These thoughts will help you manifest your birthright of happiness. Thinking positive thoughts increases your capacity to focus and allows you to improve the quality of your life. Set the intention of love and compassion and it will become your reality. Set the intention that your day will be great and it will be. Set the intention that reading this book will be a life changing experience for you and it will be.

When meditating, set an intention for your meditation. Express to yourself in words or in thought, that this is going to be an enjoyable empowering experience, and it will be. In meditation, we train our mind to cultivate a space for love. In meditation, you learn to transition from gross to more subtle feelings because of your intentions. You start by intending to feel joy, slightly transition to happiness. Subtler than happiness, you find contentment and ultimately you cultivate a space of tranquility. And it is all possible through your intention (Rick Hanson, 2009).

Next, we will go through a meditation highlighting the tools we have discussed in this section:

Peace Meditation

Seated in a comfortable posture begin to focus on your breath.

Set an intention for this meditation. What do you want to receive from this practice? It can be with words or thoughts.

Notice sounds keep happening as they always will. Revert your awareness back inside to the breath.

Imagine you are maintaining an intense focus. Think of a meditation teacher, a hero, or a religious figure, someone very focused in their spiritual practice. Now imagine you have their determined focus.

Continue focusing on your inhales and exhales as you allow your attention to sink deeper inward.

Like a puppy, you have to train the mind to sit. When you catch the mind wandering, immediately, without judgment, aim your focus back on the breath.

Notice how you are feeling and allow the sensation of joy to begin to arise. Enjoy this feeling for a moment.

Next, more subtly allow this feeling of joy to transform into happiness…

After a few moments go another level deeper to the feeling of contentment….

Give it some time and allow the transition to tranquility or peace.

Notice how quiet the mind has become.

Now your focus has become absorbed entirely in the direction of the breath. Take in the experience in its entirety and allow yourself to totally recharge.

Staying attuned to the breath, when you are ready begin to allow your peace to shift from tranquility back to contentment.

> Then to happiness…. And finally, to joy.
>
> Now come back to you everyday state of awareness.
>
> Notice how the sense of inner peace stays with you. It has always been with you on every level of your being. You only have to be aware of it to experience this overflowing sense of peace.
>
> Take three more breaths and when ready gently open your eyes.

Peace is always with you. The key is to set your intention to direct your focus on experiencing this peace. It is all too easy to get mechanically caught up in the routine of being in a rush or the need to be overly busy. It is far more rewarding to train your mind to maintain an immersion in peace. Set an intention every time you meditate that you will have an empowering experience. Set the intention from reading and practicing the techniques in this book, you will experience unprecedented development in your life. Set the intention for this lifetime to attain spiritual realization and achieve your purpose.

I remember when my Guru told me, "In this lifetime you will hit the target." Well, I am telling you now, you will achieve your goal. You will become established in peace as you realize your purpose as a divine instrument of the spirit. Like tuning into a radio station, all you must do is tune into this sense of tranquility. You see this song has always been playing inside you, but at some point our attention diverted from its highest course. Right now, set the intention to remain in tune with the song of spirit to the melody of peace. Allow yourself to receive the abundant blessings of the universe. Set the intention, continuously check to make sure you are hearing the mystical sound of harmony and enjoy the heavenly song of your life.

So, this section began, so, too, will it end with a quote from the Buddha, "As irrigators lead water to their fields, archers make their arrows straight, as carpenters carve wood, the wise shape their lives."

Peace

"Peace is not knowledge, peace is not power, peace is not happiness, but peace is all of these; and besides, peace is productive of happiness, peace inspires knowledge of the seen and unseen, and in peace is to be found the divine."
-Hazrat Inayat Khan

All men crave happiness. This quintessential craving demonstrates man's ultimate essence is happiness. Happiness comes from within, from a place of peace. The first step is every journey toward peace begins with joy. The unstable emotion of joy fluctuates constantly because it is derived externally. The nature of the material world is not constant but eternally in flux. Joy is followed by sorrow, then again comes joy, and again follows sorrow. This cycle takes place because the experience of joy manifests from a search for pleasure. The search for the illusion of pleasure results in the reality of pain. Joy is impermanent; happiness is the seat of the soul itself. The happiness I refer to is neither passing nor temporal; it is permanent because it comes from the home of stability within.

Because the search for pleasure culminates in pain, many spiritual seekers falsely believe the attainment of happiness can be manifested through the practice of renunciation. Happiness cannot be found from renunciation of worldly pleasures but from detachment to these experiences. In making the best use of these pleasures one realizes happiness comes from the truth within, from the innate essence of all beings. This essence can only be uncovered when one is alone, in silence in the seat of meditation. Having nice things or stimulating the external senses is not wrong. Worldly goods and senses exist for a reason after all. God created the physical reality as an expression of divine existence reality. Human beings are intended to experience and savor the taste of the celestial nectar. To experience this soma in its entirety one must learn to enjoy earthly pleasure with detachment from a place of presence. To be in the world but realize your source is not of the world culminates with the understanding of an unending happiness. Such a happiness sprouts the seed of contentment. When you are content, the instability in the material does not affect you. Insults and compliments, criticism and praise have no effect on one who is established in contentment. He knows an inner tranquility derived from the source, which is permanent, and beyond the influence of the vicious cycle of pleasure and pain, good or bad, right and wrong. The satisfaction of contentment is not illusory because it comes from the realization of an inner truth; you internally possess all you ever need to be happy.

At the depth of the self exists the nature of reality, the landscape of divinity and, the source of peace. When I am struggling with the discontent of the impermanent material world, I say a prayer to God to let me experience His peace. Joy, happiness, ad contentment does not create peace, but through peace all these emotions can be experienced without pain or attachment. A man who is materially wealthy may be unhappy and discontent because he does not know inner peace. A poor man may be happy and content if he possesses the spiritual wealth of life in harmony with his own internal source of peace. All that is really required is to become aware of our own innate reality, that we have always had an inherent birthright of peace.

Chapter 6: Spiritual Practice

"The inspiration of words is easier to accommodate than the perspiration of practice."
-Michael Bernard Beckwith

A student once asked my Guru during a discourse, "Why do we practice meditation?" At this question, everyone sat up in attention. We knew we were about to receive some genuine wisdom. His response, "You eat daily to feed the body. You meditate to feed the soul." Meditation allows one to nourish their very essence so their true self can be realized and brought forth to benefit the world.

What is sadhana? Sadhana is a daily spiritual practice. Every day you brush your teeth. It is the same with yoga meditation or any type of spiritual practice. You do sadhana every day to stay grounded and open to hearing what the ears cannot hear and the eyes cannot see. Spiritual practices are designed to purify the physical, emotional and spiritual bodies and allow us to de-hypnotize ourselves from the conditioning we have unconsciously been bombarded with our entire lives. There are an infinite number of different types of spiritual practices. There are innumerable types of meditations, yoga's, visualizations, and religious techniques to communicate with the divine. It is critical to find what works best for you and do it every day. Be consistent with your practice. When you cultivate a love for the practice, you discover the practice itself is the true teacher. Gurus and teachers are guides for you to find the truth within, the truth you have always known.

There are things you can do to make you spiritual practice more effective and more consistent. Find a place where you can do your practice without disruption. It may be a room in your home, a corner in your office. You may even have to move your coffee table and use your living room. What is important is that you establish and dedicate a sacred space for you practice.

Find a time that is best for you to do your practice daily. It may be early in the morning, during the day or late in the evening after work. Choose one time and do you best to stick to the schedule. In our modern lives, it can be difficult to make time for your practice. Make your practice the top priority of your day. If you do not take care of yourself first, how can you be any good for anyone else? With work, the family, and all other responsibilities, it may feel like there is not enough time in the day. I have experienced feeling this way. After dedicating myself to a daily spiritual practice, I realized how ineffectively my time was being utilized. Time will open for your sadhana and you will discover it is the most important time in your day. Your mind will function more clearly, your body will be healthier, and your intuition will be more available. All these benefits are the expression of who you really are. When you walked into a room as your true self, without any conditioning, you will cause waves of consciousness to shift in all those around you.

The quality of your commitment determines your level of success in meditation. Michael Bernard Beckwith's statement holds true here, "To the spiritually mature, commitment is the equivalent of freedom because it bestows authentic happiness that cannot be taken away" (Beckwith, 2008). Depending on your schedule, you may have to change the time of your practice from day to day. This is okay and may only be temporary. The important thing is that you do your sadhana every day no matter what. You would not go a day without brushing your teeth. You would not go a day without eating. Then how could you ever go a day without practicing your meditation?

Before you sit down to practice, create some rituals. You may appreciate the act of lighting a candle or incense. Does it feel right to turn the lights off or cover the windows? Find what you need to do to make the environment feel conducive to your meditation. Practicing these rituals are like tying knots that effectively maintain the energy of your daily sadhana.

In your meditation space, you may enjoy and benefit from creating an altar. You can place pictures of people or places that inspire you. You could place flowers or crystals in the space. As I said earlier, candles and incense are great complements to your practice. I like burning sweet grass incense or sage to purify the energy in the room. Keep the area spotlessly clean. An unclean space is not fit for meditation. When the area is unorganized, it will give your mind more to dwell on. It is another distraction to divert your attention.

There will be days when you just do not feel like coming to your yoga mat, meditation pillow, or prayer space. It is my experience that these are the days when you learn the most about yourself, and when you have the biggest breakthroughs, or aha moments. Your desire to veer away from your practice usually comes from issues in your subconscious that you are avoiding. You avoid them because they are uncomfortable. But remember, nothing grows or changes in comfortable circumstances. Why would it? Discomfort is the catalyst for our personal growth. This is the beauty of daily sadhana. It's something you must do whether you want to or not, but you do it because you understand the invaluable longterm benefits of the practice.

There may be times when you experience intense emotional swings in life, extreme highs or lows. These moments are the most difficult and the most beneficial times to meditate. Your practice gives you the ability to find your center and have insight into your difficulties and successes. When you are in an emotional valley, do whatever it takes to get out of that stagnation. When you are at an emotional peak, recognize what you did to get there and keep doing what it takes to stay there. Meditation teaches that nothing is permanent in life and allows us to be compassionate to ourselves throughout our trials. The mind has the tendency to create judgments about others and ourselves. Mediation allows us to disconnect from these judgments and understand they are not true. We are not our thoughts. Learning to use discernment without judging others and ourselves is an additional benefit of the meditation practice.

How do you make the mind more fertile for meditation?

You make the mind more fertile for meditation by understanding and utilizing the dynamics of vibration. At the essence of our core we are vibration. The human body is made of organs made of cells made of atoms made of molecules made of light photons ultimately comprised of vibrations. Everyone runs on a certain frequency. Some people's frequencies are geared more toward survival or pleasure. Other's vibrations are more tuned into compassion or creativity. Some are more attuned to spirit. There are an infinite number of different frequencies that are all generated from a specific intention. Connecting your frequency with God is the highest intention. Many people fluctuate back and forth through the range of frequency. When you connect with the divine frequency, the infinite will become evident and possible to identify.

Your personal frequency is heightened by your meditation practice. Your intention helps to define your tone. The external vibrations around us effect our vibrations. Listening to music is an example of how external vibrations influence our internal vibrations. Peaceful or serene music resonates with your peaceful, harmonious vibrations. Heavy, angry music makes you feel unsettled and upset. Action movies make you feel tense, while loves stories encourage you to connect to a place of compassion in your heart. Watching too much news tends to make one feel crazy and depressed. Being around a spiritual person or community of people heightens your spiritual vibration. Being around friends who overdrink tends to encourage you to overindulge. Reading sacred texts and visiting beautiful places in nature are great ways to increase your connection and heighten your vibration.

Ask yourself what are some examples of things that heighten and lower the tone you set in your life? The people around us, television or music we subscribe to, the amount of time spent in nature, the type of food we eat, all affect our personal vibration. These are all examples of external sensory stimulation. They are things that stimulate the grossest part of our spiritual selves. The spiritual practice creates more awareness of the subtler layers of the self.

Your sadhana stimulates your internal senses. Awareness of your breath, stability of your emotions, understanding of your intellect and knowledge of your true self are the internal senses experienced by turning your awareness inward. To change your life, it is easiest to start working on the qualities you can transform. You cannot change the world around you without changing the world inside first. Working on your inner self is how you make a lasting impact on the physical world.

It is possible to get to a point where your internal frequency is so great that you have more of an influence on the external world than vice versa. This comes with knowledge, devotion, and action. The external world can drain your spiritual energy. It is important to know when it is time to withdraw your senses and recharge. An enlightened person understands that balancing internal and external energies keeps the battery of the soul fully charged with spirit.

Training the mind with meditation is like training a puppy to stay. You must keep reminding the puppy to sit. So, too, with the mind we must keep reminding it to come back to focusing on the breath, mantra, or other technique you may be using. When you catch your mind wandering, mentally tap yourself on the shoulder and bring awareness back to the meditation. Avoid judging yourself and you will recognize this is all part of the process. Be patient and compassionate with yourself. You will find that with consistent practice the quality and benefits of your meditation will consistently improve.

A Guru teaches from the authentic viewpoint of an enlightened being. An enlightened person has such heightened vibrations that his or her internal vibrations have more of an effect on the external world. I love my Guru's analogy comparing churning milk into butter to becoming enlightened. Once butter has formed it will never go back to milk. The same is true with enlightenment. Once you know truth, you can never go back to ignorance. This does not mean once you are enlightened all issues of modern life just go away. With heightened awareness comes the ability to monitor the fluctuations of your internal energy. This is like knowing how full or empty your cup is when you come to the dinner table. When your cup gets low, you go to the kitchen to refill it. Enlightenment is knowing when it is time to fill your cup before it empties and your energy is depleted. The action of filling your cup is analogous to your sadhana and the practice of meditation.

When I would talk to my Guru about worldly issues concerning my living arrangements, love life, and power struggles at work, he would give me the guidance I needed. In the process, his energy would slowly start to be drained. The issues I wanted to discuss were all matters of the lower chakras. It is all too easy to get caught up in the melodrama of our contemporary lives. He would tell me, "Ask me about meditation?" in an attempt to heighten the vibration of our discussion. Bringing the conversation to a higher chakra, he transformed our vibration and reorienting the flow of our energy toward a higher dimension. The demands of modern life can be draining. It is very important to traverse the proving ground of consciousness with awareness. By paying attention to the fluctuations of energy within you, you can assure the vehicle of your consciousness stays full of the fuel needed to empower your development.

Daily sadhana is critical for anyone on the path to enlightenment. You have to have enough gas in the tank to make it to your destination. Sadhana gives you the ability to be aware and monitor the level of your energetic gas tank. When it is full, when you are overflowing with divine energy give it back to the world, serve others. But serve with awareness. Make the journey, but monitor the level of your gas tank as if you were making a cross-country drive. When your fuel gauge shows you are starting to get low on spiritual fuel anytime during the day, withdraw, go into a moment of silence. Refill your energetic tank with meditation.

You cannot fill a gas tank that is already full. The best way to use your spiritual gas is service. Serving others from your heart requires the use of your spiritual energy, and serving humbly in this way simultaneously keeps your tank full. Be discerning about how you use your energy throughout the day. After spending time alone in meditation, you feel blissful. Reentering into the material world can have an adverse effect on our bliss. Certain people, places and things will keep your battery charged. Certain things will drain your battery. Pay close attention to these things and continuously monitor the level of your energy.

As you heighten your vibration, you begin to have a great effect on the world around you. This effect may be evident in a gross or subtle way. It may be serving food to 500 people a day in a soup kitchen. It may be teaching spiritual principals to influential people in your community. We each have our own way, our own purpose. What is important is that you find your specific purpose and live it. The world needs more people to realize their divine purpose so we can transform the planet, and most importantly improve our impact on the environment. A global change is coming whether we want to accept it or not. Individually we cannot stop change, but we can shape the type of change that will happen. Our individual choices and actions directly influence the collective transformation.

The fact change is coming makes sadhana ever so much more important. Heightened consciousness will give the global community the awareness required to live in harmony with the planet. The earth's energetic gas tank is quickly becoming depleted. Sadhana gives the individual and the collective the ability to replenishment the planet's energy. We all have individual choices to make on momentary basis that will affect the planet on a global scale. Should I walk or drive? Should I question where my food comes from or how is it made? Is it permissible to just buy all my food at the grocery store and not consider such details? Do I replant grass this season or should I research more environmentally friendly method of landscaping? We all have the means to create change. The overwhelming majority of us just do not know it yet.

Most people consciously choose to keep living in the dark. It is time to awaken. Turn the television off. Reconnect to nature. Check out of living a materialistic lifestyle and tune into reality. Stop letting consumer marketing hypnotize you and become more conscious about spending habits. The way we spend money affects us karmically. If we spend money on diamonds for a wedding ring that were mined by forced labor in war torn countries, and intend those gemstones to represent eternal love for a spouse, what does that say about the energy being put into of the relationship? Perhaps this has something to do with the 50 percent divorce rate in the United States. When we spend money on goods created by immoral actions we are condoning those actions. Much of the goods we use in the West are created using child labor. When we support these actions by dedicating the fruits of our labor toward those practices, we are technically financing this methodology.

Become entirely accountable for your actions and do not allow the disease of ignorance to manifest in your life.

A beginning level enlightened person is said to have influence over an area with a diameter of 500 miles. A high level enlightened person can affect the entire planet. A candle in a dark room spreads its light like knowledge overcomes ignorance. Darkness cannot overtake light. The world needs more light. Sadhana keeps the fire lit, and consistent practice turns your flame into a torch. It is time to enlighten the planet. We can only make this transformation if we do it together.

Silence

The trees, the flowers, the plants grow in silence. The stars, the sun, the moon, move in silence. Silence gives us a new perspective.

-Mother Theresa

The old adage, "Silence is golden," could not be more true or profound. Silence is more precious than gold, especially in our society. As we have discussed before in previous sections, at our biological root, we are vibration. The vibrations we take in and put out affect us tremendously. The thoughts we maintain determine the way we see others and ourselves. Why in the world would we want to handicap others or ourselves by creating boundaries to greatness with self-limiting ideas? People in our culture are incredibly unaware of how the things they think and say affect the world around them. Many individuals are so unaware of what they say, it appears they have contracted a case of verbal diarrhea. If you do not believe me, visit a bar or crowded restaurant during a football game. Sit in silence and observe what people are saying. The truncated level of consciousness will blow your mind.

To heighten consciousness of what you think and say, I recommend a simple meditation practice, be silent! First try this for an hour. Next try it 24 hours. It may seem impossible and you may need to arrange your schedule to accommodate the practice but I assure you it is entirely possible and surprisingly refreshing, both physically and mentally. Maybe you can work your way up to staying in silence for three days or even a week.

Keep a note pad with you to communicate with those around you without speaking. The Indian saint Anandamayi Ma stayed in silence for three years! My Guru, Yogi Shivraj, maintained his silence for six months to heighten his personal vibration. Speaking to him after he came out of silence, receiving his Shakti pot (divine transmission) was both humbling and electrifying. The clarity he expressed was an unmatched experience in my lifetime.

This is the same reason Yogis go into caves in India to meditate. The dense molecular structure of the rock keeps harmful vibrations out and the positive vibrations created by meditation in. Chanting mantras silently during your time in silence is a powerful way to improve the quality of your experience.

Maintaining an extended period of silence heightens your sensitivity to sound. You will realize how beneficial, or detrimental the people around you really are. Your awareness of how external vibrations influence your energy skyrockets. In silence, it becomes easier to meditate and to escalate your spiritual vibrations. Try this practice for a predetermined amount of time and you will be amazed at how the relationship you have with yourself improves.

Alone – All One

To be alone is the most beautiful place in existence. It is so healthy, so beneficial for your development. To be alone is different from isolation. Separating yourself from others in isolation is a lonely experience. Isolation from your true reality, the reality of God in you, this is the cause of loneliness.

Aloneness is a state of higher consciousness. Look at the word alone. When we break it down we have two words, "all" and "one". When we are alone we are uncontaminated by the thoughts of others. It is possible to discover in yourself a state of clarity, a state of oneness. You can be around many people and feel totally isolated and lonely.

Once I found myself in a group of negative people. When I finally found the opportunity to leave that group and be alone, I said a prayer. I asked God to help me improve my outlook on life, to find peace. My thoughts and understanding of life had been contaminated by the negativity around me. My prayer was quickly answered. A positive person came around and we could heighten each other's energy as one. When I was in the negative group of many people, I felt as isolated and separated from God as ever. When I found time and space to be alone, I could reconnect to my source.

Later that day I had more time to be alone and indulge in the contemplative practice of my yoga asana. The practice seemed challenging at first, but I realized this was because I had allowed my thought process to be polluted. Deciding to reverse the flow of energy, I started telling myself the practice was easy, and it quickly seemed to become easy. The challenging sequence of yoga postures was over before I knew it. This mental practice is a great sequence to happiness. Prapitaka Bhavana, cultivating the opposite state of mind, allowed me to overcome the feeling of discontent I had been experiencing. Life is beautiful, flowing with ease.

When life seems challenging and you tell yourself things are hard, they will be. It does not matter why you believe these things are hard. It could be based on past experiences or from considering the influence of others. It could be due to attachment, aversion or fears that all come from some form of ignorance. Whatever the reason, practice cultivating the opposite train of thought. Create the state of mind to maintain the awareness that things are easy, fun and beautiful, and they will be. When you spend time alone, you can connect to the source of all things, the reality of all nature. God is in you. You are enlightened. You just didn't know it yet, but now you do. The problem is we are easily confused. Others easily contaminate our mental process. Therefore, it is so important to spend time alone with God in deep meditation. When you spend time alone, it creates the vacuum needed to recharge your spiritual energy, to clarify every layer of yourself.

The deeper you get into your daily spiritual practice, the more you will begin to enjoy the sacredness of your time alone. You will not be isolating yourself. You will not feel lonely, because you will be connecting to your true self. It is like plugging your power cord into the source for all energy. Spend time alone, in meditation or silence on a regular basis. Aloneness is your opportunity to participate in a cosmic energy transmission, renewing purity of your divine self. As you learn to be comfortable alone, you learn to get your life right with God. Approach this experience with joy and you will know peace in your heart.

Selfless Service

"You give little when you give of your possessions; it is when you give of yourself that you truly give"

"The Prophet" By Kahlil Gibran

Seva is a beautiful concept. It means to serve someone, God, a teacher, student, family member, friend, stranger, or anyone and expect nothing in return. It is very important for the spiritual seeker to renounce the fruits of his or her labor. When one realizes his or her actions are only accomplished by adhering to the will of the divine, it becomes easier to offer the harvest of their labor as an offering to God. It takes great humility to serve God removing the ego's desire from the equation.

When you act in service only for the self it is action derived from ignorance. Ignorance is blanketed by the veil of illusion. The illusion of duality, the notion that the individual is separate from the whole. This notion is entirely untrue. All human beings are a single entity in a larger organism designed to function in harmony. Separating yourself from the whole creates symptoms of disease. The ego creates these false beliefs. When we act in selfless service for others, we overcome the intoxication of the ego. Through a deeper understanding achieved by undertaking your spiritual work, clarity of one's individual purpose in the larger scheme of things becomes evident. The most expedient path to enlightenment is through selfless service. Tuning into the vibrational field of the heart guides us to our specific task in service of the whole. When you serve others in the manner of your purpose, it does not drain your energy. You do not get tired from it. Seva recharges your spiritual body and energizes every dimension of yourself.

I recall teaching a yoga and meditation workshop in San Luis, Mexico. The commute to the yoga studio took three hours (each way) from San Diego. I left my home at five in the morning and did not return until nearly midnight. When I arrived at the studio, the large yoga community graciously welcomed me. Everyone was so grateful and eager to learn. I was not at all there with the specific intent of making money. I was there as an act of seva for my Guru, to spread his message, to share the beauty of rising in love through the practice of yoga.

Time was nonexistent throughout the day. It seemed the workshop ended too soon. No one, including myself wanted to leave. The group energy was just magical. We took a picture with 40 people. I was in the middle and every person in the picture physically touched some part of my body to reinforce the energetic connection of the gathering. As I write now, the thought of that day nearly brings tears to my eyes. That day I truly experienced unconditional love and it was the energy of abundance that left my heart overflowing. Throughout my drive home, I felt incredibly energized. When I finally made it home, I realized, despite having worked very hard all day beginning early in the morning, I felt neither thirst nor hunger at any time throughout the day.

    Through selfless service, we are energized on every level from our physical body to our spiritual karma. Logically, it does not make sense that serving others can satisfy hunger, but this was truly my experience and it has happened to me on multiple occasions. We are metaphysical beings. Metaphysical means beyond the understanding of mind and body. If the divine can feed our soul, why would It not be able to feed the more gross aspects of the self like the mind and body? Seva is a beautiful experience. You can practice seva (selfless service) and receive a great deal in return. Your sankalpa (intention) in the performance of your task determines whether your act is selfless or not. Are you performing this task for personal benefit or are your actions entirely altruistic, with great devotion for the benefit of others?

    No one acts without serving the self on some level. Even in seva, serving with the intention to get closer to God is still serving yourself in a way. There is truth in this statement but allow me to expand. Most people preform a task that is not what I define as seva when their motivation comes from the ego. When our lower energy centers dictate our personal desire, the action is not selfless. There is a difference in serving the lower and higher selves. Serving the lower self is being under the control of the ego. In this sense, operating from the ego, one performs an action because of a misconception based on an illusion. The illusion is that every being is not connected and we should struggle to outdo each other. Working at a job where you do not feel you make a difference in the world solely to earn money just to pay the bills and get by until the next paycheck is an example of operating from the lower self.

Serving from a place of the heart, serving the higher energy centers, serving others in divine purpose is what is meant by seva. Serving the divine in your own self is what is meant by seva. What is meant by the self, the sense of "me" or "mine", is a distorted perception of reality. The idea that you are separate from everyone else is simply untrue. All life is interconnected. Man is not the entire web of life; he is merely a single strand of it.

Seva is really service of your true self; service from the heart for the world. When you accept the necessity of primal energies like basic survival needs, pleasure, and individual struggles for power, you begin to serve the spirit in you. By creatively serving your heart and adhering to your intuition, you access the guidance of spirit. You are the spirit. This is the real you. This inner divine space in you, your highest self, is accessed by serving the well-being of others. When you act in this manner, things seem to flow without effort. Miracles happen when you overcome the ego and surrender to the ultimate will. Then you are serving the true you, the reality of God in you. This is what is meant by seva, serving the highest aspect of your self.

Gandhi said, "One who would serve will not waste a thought upon his own comforts, which leaves to be attended to or neglected by his Master on high. He will not, therefore, encumber himself with everything that comes his way; he will take only what he strictly needs and leave the rest. He will be calm, free from anger and unruffled in mind even if he finds himself inconvenienced. His service, like virtue, is its own reward, and he will rest content with it."

Gandhi was a true spiritual revolutionary. He embodied selfless service. Through his example, we are given action steps on how to entirely put the needs of others before our own. By not wasting any efforts on his own indulgence, he put all effort into attaining his goal by serving others. He required the bare minimum for himself, which allowed him to devote all his energy to the well-being of others. He found joy in devoting total effort to his cause. In doing so, he tapped into an insurmountable power. Such a determination allows the practitioner to experience an overwhelming sense of peace and tranquility.

In true Gandhian fashion (as it was his beloved script) I will quote Krishna in the Bhagavad Gita (Easwaran, Essence of the Bhagavad Gita, 2011):

Just as fire is covered by smoke and a mirror is covered by dust, just as the embryo rests deep within the womb, knowledge is hidden by selfish desire.

By serving others altruistically, expecting nothing in return, you receive more than you could ever imagine. Through selfless service, you tap into a source with the power to move mountains, an understanding of universal truth, and an unending endurance, which enables you to realize your purpose.

I end this chapter with an adaptation of a meditation popularized by Saint Francis of Assisi. This meditation has been modified and used by all faiths. At one point in the meditation, Francis guided the practitioner to utilize the image of Christ. Depending on your religious background (or lack thereof) you can use a different manifestation of the divine. If you are a Hindu, you can channel Krishna or any other form of God. If you are a Muslim, use Mohammed. If you are Jewish, you can channel Moses, Abraham or even God Himself. Choose the vision of your Higher Power to work with. If you are agnostic or atheist, complete this practice with the universal energy or divine order. The meditation can be adapted to all belief systems.

> **St Francis' Meditation**
>
> Begin by tuning into your breathing. Take three deep breaths. Continue focusing on your breathing.
>
> Now as you inhale breath in Christ, or any manifestation of God as you understand Him. Allow the sensation of God to permeate deep within you
>
> As you exhale, breathe out all negative energy you have been holding onto.
>
> Next picture the image of your Higher Power wrapping his or her arms around you, hugging you in a loving embrace. Continue breathing consciously here for a few minutes.
>
> As you breathe, inhale and exhale the energy of peace. Peace is divine. God manifested is peace. Work with the most powerful force in the universe connecting to peace through your breath. Breath in the peace of the universe and as your exhale create peace in the world.
>
> Return to focusing on your normal breathing. Take three more deep breaths and when ready slowly begin to open your eyes.

The divine is all around us, without and within. This energy permeates every molecule of your being as well as all of creation. In meditation, you connect to the universal essence and align yourself with peace and become grounded. Everyone deserves to know the truth. It is your birthright. You owe it to yourself to connect to this reality with meditation.

Some forms of meditation encourage the practitioner to empty the mind and still all thoughts. Other forms are guided and encourage the utilization of images, emotions, and energy. All forms of meditation are good and improve one's ability to focus and concentrate on higher aspects of the self, taking us deeper into the present moment. The here and now is all there is. When I contemplate the future, fear and worry arise. In the here and now, I have ability to connect to the empowering energy of peace. Peace is the energy that guides the universe. Everything else is just a temporary illusion. Peace is everlasting. The famous prayer of Saint Francis begins, "Lord make me an instrument of thy peace." In the material world truth is hidden and can only be uncovered by connecting to our innate reality of inner peace. The great yearning for enlightenment comes from the desire to know an immense, indescribable tranquility. The practice of meditation will take you there.

Chapter 7: Developing the Right Attitude

"Strength, if it is spiritual, is a power for spiritual realization; a greater power is sincerity, the greatest power is grace."

-Sri Aurobindo

There are three very important attitudes that can be utilized in the progression of our spiritual journey. Attitude determines your ability to move with grace through the air of spirituality.

Physical and spiritual strength are two very different qualities. Physical strength is having a strong body, the ability to manipulate matter by means of the muscular system. Spiritual strength is of an internal nature. It is an aptitude for having a determination in seeking the soul. When one is spiritually strong, he or she utilizes that resilience to endure the challenges of life, to concentrate and cultivate the control of focus required to create a meditation. Physical strength is a rudimentary element of the body. Spiritual strength is used for progression on the journey of the seeker. Although strength is a basic quality, it is a critical tool for developing deeper more subtle qualities on your expedition toward realization of the self. Use your stamina and determination to concentrate and focus. Use an appropriate effort and eventually you will learn to utilize the heroic determination within. This will take you deeper. You will be able to spend more time in meditation and maintain concentration.

At one point strength alone is no longer a sufficient attitude for the spiritual aspirant. This is where your level of sincerity becomes critically important. Strength can only take you so far. Use your strength as much as you can, but eventually you will come to a barrier preventing your progression. This is where you ask yourself, "How badly do I want it?" "How sincere am I?" I find great relevance in the idea that to realize the self, you must want to find God like a drowning man wants air.

The quality of your sincerity is determined by the truth of your intention. Why are you on this path? What are you looking for? Is your goal to satisfy the craving of the ego for power or to achieve liberation of the soul? Like the dying man and air, the nature of the ego is to satisfy its need for earthly desire. The nature of the soul is to satisfy its desire for union with the divine.

There are two main characters in the great Indian epic, "The Ramayana". The protagonist is Rama and the villain, or antagonist is Ravana. (Interestingly enough, Ravana is where we get the English word for ravenous). In the tale, Rama is a divine incarnation. Ravana was the most powerful ruler on the face of the earth. To satisfy his desire for pleasure, Ravana kidnaps Rama's beautiful wife Sita. The plot is filled with Rama's journey as he follows his dharma (path to God or duty) to retrieve Sita from the evil demon king. The main characters of the story are excellent examples of the depth of sincerity required by the spiritual seeker. Ravana's desires are to fulfill the needs of the physical body. He craves money, sex, and power. Rama's focus is solely to follow the will of God, to do what is right. (Take this opportunity to ask yourself, "What inspires me? What motivates me? Are my motives egotistical or spiritual?")

Rama's hardships seem only to strengthen his resolve. His purest of intentions demonstrate the depth of his sincerity. This level of sincerity leads to something greater. In a very subtle manner, it leads to grace. Grace is a divine expression, a spiritual experience. Grace gives us the ability to see the synchronicity in our lives. We realize the interconnectedness of the big picture of God's plan for us. By maintaining a place of peace in our hearts, we are guided by divine grace on God's path.

Returning to the Ramayana, after Sita's kidnapping, Rama is tormented by grief. He searches high and low but is unable to find her. Abiding by his dharma (duty), with great devotion to his wife, Rama is guided in meeting the hero of the story, Hanuman, the embodiment of grace. Hanuman is known for his incredible strength. He becomes sincerely devoted to Rama's cause and eventually helps him find and rescue Sita. I'll leave you here to do your own deeper investigations into the tale of the Ramayana. I recommend the versions translated by Ramesh Menon and William Buck.

Strength and sincerity are invaluable tools on the path to enlightenment. Practice using these tools, develop the devotion required to experience grace. With patience, we travel the road of devotion and realize we are surrounded by grace. Grace is serendipitous. With grace, your life seems to flourish by happenstance, but nothing happens by chance. We are guided entirely by the divine. Strength is necessary to begin our journey. It allows us to purify our intention and cultivate pure sincerity. Grace guides us the rest of the way home (Aurobindo, 1995).

The epic of the Ramayana is an excellent metaphor for understanding the metaphysical being. Rama represents the spiritual chakra. His wife Sita represents the earthly root chakra. The two nodes meet by the grace of Hanuman, who represents the breath (which is rather appropriate as Hanuman is the son of the wind). In our lives, we connect the physical and the spirit world through the grace of the breath. Tuning into your breathing allows you to slow the body and mind, heightening the spiritual vibration. This gives you the ability to tune into the frequency of the inner world. See to your spiritual practice with strength and sincerity and you will recognize the divine grace ever present in your life.

A friend once told me, "I'm interested in learning about spirituality, but I'm just not that into God." I told him, "That does not mean God is not that into you." With grace, we realize that part of ourselves that has always been there. We were just not yet aware of it. Christ taught us to listen without our ears and see without the eyes. Living in the inner world we can find the connection between the head and the heart. You learn to recognize your own truth instead of living by the rules and laws imposed by others. This is the ultimate freedom, an expression of perfection. When we tune into the vibrations of the spirit we gain the ability to see the true, faultless self.

Suffering

"Now and then I go about pitying myself and all the while my soul is being blown by great winds across the sky."

Obijiway Native American Saying

Obstacles are opportunities to be steadfast. In these occasions, make the commitment to never give away the infinite power of peace. In suffering lies such a great blessing, such a great opportunity. The connotation of words with ideas, in many cases, represents the mechanization of our thought process over the millennia. The process of enlightenment is a system of de-mechanization, deconditioning, or dehypnotization of the mind.

Suffering offers the opportunity for growth. In the momentary experience of suffering, we develop tunnel vision and completely lose perspective of the bigger picture. Often in life we chase short- term pleasure and experience long-term pain. The enlightened mind understands short- term pain (in the appropriate circumstances) results in long-term pleasure. Just think of all the instances in your life when you were forced to go through suffering. These experiences result in the culmination of strength not only in body but also in will and spirit.

Think about the connotation associated with the idea of suffering. Then you will understand the truth of the teaching of the Buddha, "The path to enlightenment is through suffering." If suffering leads to enlightenment, then suffering is a good thing. Should we not welcome suffering as we would we would welcome a friend who is offering assistance? Suffering and the ego offer us a great paradox. Suffering is created by the ego and ultimately the acceptance of suffering dissolves the ego (Tolle, 2005).

Relationships

When we end an unhealthy romantic relationship, there is an intense aversion to suffering. We think many unrealistic emotional thoughts like, "I'm going to be alone", "He or she is going to find someone else", or "I'll never be in love again". All these thoughts are fallacies. Yes, there will be suffering, but to be in love, you must allow yourself to be vulnerable to being hurt. Ending the unhealthy relationship is taking your first step to transforming the suffering. You cannot truly love someone else until you learn to love yourself. You usually have to hit the reset button and learn to do this all on your own. When a relationship ends going through emotional suffering strengthens and broadens the nature of your understanding of love.

My Guru taught that we should not fall in love. Falling literally means bringing you down. We should rise in love. Rising in love with another person means you are raising each other to a higher spiritual dimension. Together you are heightening each other's vibrations. You complement each other and the relationship naturally encourages the other's evolution. We should all aspire to creating and maintaining relationships of this nature. Seek out relationships that guide you toward divine communion. The healthiest romantic relationship is the one in which both partners are oriented toward the light. Here I am describing a spiritually fulfilling relationship with another human being. Remember it is impossible to find what only God can give you in another human being. Both people do not have to be meditators but it helps when the other accommodates and compliments your spiritual practice. In this way by connecting with your life partner in the physical realm, the soul is guided toward its source in the spiritual realm.

Experiencing the suffering of separating from a partner gives you the opportunity to connect with someone else in another relationship where you can rise in love. When you leave a relationship what is suffering is your ego, your sense of control over another person. Let it go. Do not wish ill of another. Realize you got what you needed at one time from the relationship. With an appreciation for the other, send them on their journey and in turn you will be able to continue yours. Do not cling to attachment. Let them be free and you will find freedom yourself. Embrace the experience. Suffering is the soil for you to plant and germinate the seeds of change.

My dear friend and yoga teacher Natasha explained relationships to me in a unique way. Spending too much time and energy on a non-working relationship is like overwatering a flower in a garden. If you over water a single flower, that flower will wilt and eventually die. Instead of giving all the water to the single flower, spread the water around the garden and give attention to all the flowers. When you put all your energy into saving a non-working relationship, it becomes the wilting flower. Instead of wasting all your energy and creating emotional turmoil, spread your love around to all the beautiful people in your life. Spend time with friends, family, and teachers. Immerse yourself in the strength of community. Be the water bearer for love instead of emotional turmoil. This practice will make your transition in life much more peaceful, enjoyable, and painless.

Work

Losing a job, we go through much suffering. Financially, it can be devastating. What is hurt the most is our ego. We begin asking ourselves questions like, "Am I not good enough to do this job?" or, "Someone else is better than I am?" In all honesty, it was probably not the right job for you and the divine has bigger plans. Dream bigger. Follow your heart. What do you truly want to do in your life that allows you to be of greater service to the world? As we are learning and growing it is often necessary to take a lesser than desired position until you fully realize the skills you need to obtain your dream job. Play each role to the best of your ability and do not become attached when it is necessary to move onward and upward. It also helps to maintain a mindset of gratitude for having a job in the first place. Make a shift from the debilitating stance of victimhood to more empowering attitudes of leadership and personal excellence.

Dealing with Death

There are few obstacles in life I can recollect in which people find greater challenge

than dealing with the death of a loved one. Before I cover this topic, I must mention the practice of these principles are much more difficult to practice than to understand in theory, even for me.

Attachment to a loved one is great. When distinguishing the difference between love and attachment, we must ask ourselves if it would be possible to live without the person. In attachment, you cannot live without the person. In love, you miss the person, but even without them physically in your life, the experience of knowing them has left you a better person and you can appreciate their contribution to your life.

When you remember a lost loved one, keep your thoughts are based on love, not attachment. Recall the memories you appreciated for having the person in your life. Remember the things you were grateful for about them. Wish the person well and know they have merely made a transition from one stage of their soul's journey to the next. The body is just a vehicle for the soul. When your car gets old, you trade it in for a newer more appropriate car. It is the same with our bodies. The human body has a finite lifespan unlike the infinite lifecycle of the soul. When the body wears out, the soul transitions to the next more appropriate vehicle for its development. It is not easy to accept this universal cycle when we are grieving. Allow yourself time, compassion, and ultimately acceptance.

Know this instance of suffering like all others, is designed to encourage your own personal evolution. The sooner we accept the natural transition of death, the sooner we can shift our sadness, grief and despair, to love, appreciation and gratitude for the magnificent soul we were blessed to encounter. You may not understand why things must be the way they are right now, but know that you will meet them again. In one moment, you will understand why things had to be the way they were. Love will keep you constantly connected to those have passed. All the other mixed emotions you may experience only distort your connection to them.

Suffering as a Spiritual Experience

Most of us begin our spiritual journey because of an intense experience of suffering. The most empowering approach is to be grateful for the experience. It gives you a tremendous opportunity for transformation and you can take advantage of the prospect.

I have already told my story about being sent to a boarding school when I was in high school. When I returned home, I was fill with anger and pain. I consciously chose to sever my spiritual connection. I denied all faith in the idea of a divine order, ceasing to believe in God altogether. I only compounded my problems using drugs.

At one point, to express my anger, I decided the best thing for me would be to get into mixed martial arts fighting. I began to do some background research on Brazilian Jiu-Jitsu and surprisingly learned the most successful adherents to art practiced yoga to gain balance, strength, flexibility, and improve proprioception (awareness of one's place in space). Watching interviews with champions, it seemed all the martial artists who practiced yoga knew a degree of peace unknown to me.

    One night my mother introduced me to yogic breathing through the practice of pranayama. It was like some meditations I had done before with a heightened awareness to controlling the breath. From my first conscious breath, I experienced a heightened awareness and reconnected to a sacred place in myself. Beginning a spiritual journey inward, I started the journey to return to my true self. This deep breathing practice led to the more physically intense Ashtanga Yoga practice. This eventually led to a powerful and consistent meditation practice. These disciplines entirely changed my life from the inside out. I rediscovered a place of peace that had been there all along.

Through my suffering, anger, and pain, all I wanted to do was fight. These experiences and emotions were the expression of divine guidance through the universal order guiding me home. Suffering turned to surrender. Anger transformed to love, and pain became peace. The process did not happen overnight. After beginning my journey inward, I continued to face emotional fluctuations and make the wrong decisions most of the time. The transformations process has been a gradual one.

    Negative emotions are God's way of guiding us back to the positive ones. Without pain, there could not be peace. Without hate, there could be no love. Without feeling an absence of God in our lives, why would we begin a search in the first place? What is this sense of longing and absence? It is nothing more than the call to turn inward. Suffering creates a yearning for God. Without one there could not be the other.

Pain is a guide to peace. The universe truly works in mysterious ways. Darkness is needed to experience the glory of light. The more harmonious emotions such as peace and love are the expression of the divine in us. Anger, pain, fear, and the like are the divine call of the spirit to search inward, to return home.

Control to Surrender

"Suffering has a noble purpose: the evolution of consciousness and the burning up of the ego"

-Eckhart Tolle

The fight for control is one of the greatest causes of suffering. We all want to feel empowered and most mistake the illusion of control for empowerment. Control is nothing more than another mode of the ego. We think we are in control of our reality when our lives are a playing field to advance our spiritual development.

Advancement is not about learning how to control (which we all already know how to do). Advancing forward in your spiritual journey is only possible through surrender. Control is merely an illusion. Surrender is the path of humility.

Often in life, we believe we know what is best for us, or we know exactly what we want when God or the universal order expresses other desires. Let's imagine, you have been saving to go on a fancy vacation. It has taken you nearly six months but you finally have all the money you need for the vacation when you get a letter from the IRS saying you have underpaid your taxes. The amount you underpaid on your taxes was the exact amount you had saved for your vacation. The IRS is ordering you to pay the remainder of your taxes immediately. This situation is a good example of how we are not always in control of the material world that governs our physical life. It is impossible to control the physical realm. All we can really control is our emotional response to the material reality.

Attempting to control the situation with the IRS would only cause emotional suffering. Nothing can really be done to change the situation. Fighting to control the circumstances in the physical world would only create a struggle within the emotional self. Fighting for control usually manifests as anger, frustration, or discontent. This does not sound like a very healthy emotional state.

What would surrender look like in this situation? Gratitude is a miraculous step toward surrender. You may ask, "What is there to be grateful about in this situation?" You could be grateful you had saved the money and can pay the remainder of your taxes in this first place. Unfortunately, the vacation must wait, but the fact you had the money saved to cover the balance is a cause for gratitude. Imagine where you would be if you received the letter from the IRS the week after you returned from your vacation. You would realize you were blessed to receive the letter when you did and be thankful you had the ability to pay the taxes.

Nothing that happens in this world is outside the realm of a greater universal order, even if we cannot see it from our point of view at the time. Our setbacks in life are most often the setups for our greatest achievements. Instead of fighting our challengers, we should learn to surrender to them, even find a sense of gratitude for them. Now you can begin to see your unique individual path toward success. Your challenges are meant to strengthen you for the journey ahead. Invite your challenges and now they are tests designed to teach you lessons you will utilize in the future.

Surrender is the path of least resistance. Imagine a sailboat in the ocean. The sailboat can only navigate in the direction of the wind. It does not travel against the wind very effectively. When the captain of the vessel surrenders to the wind, he gains the ability to overcome the ocean waves and navigate the destined course. In this analogy, you are the sailboat, God's will or desire for you is the wind and our world is the ocean. When you fight the wind (the divine will) you are pummeled by wave after wave of life. When you surrender to the divine will, you find the energy to overcome the waves and navigate your chosen course.

Some misinterpret surrender for giving up. There is a yoga sutra that states "Sthira sukham asanam". The most direct translation is, "Yoga postures should be practiced with appropriate effort and appropriate surrender". Just because you surrender does not mean you give up and stop trying. You need to be honest enough with yourself to understand the moments when effort or surrender is appropriate. When your taxes were due, yes you should surrender to the fact that you must pay them, but do not lose hope of your vacation. Keep working and saving money because you will get your vacation when the timing is right.

To navigate a sailboat on the open ocean requires a great deal of effort. But it is only possible when you surrender to the current of the wind. Work hard when it is appropriate to work hard and surrender when it is appropriate to surrender. Certain yoga postures require you to use strength in one muscle group and find flexibility in others. This is life. Some areas you need to be strong, in some areas you need to be flexible. Life is balance. Find strength through surrender. Travel the middle path. This is the journey to merge with the will of the divine.

Chapter 8: Faith

Be aware of me always, adore me, make every act an offering to me, and you shall come to me. This I promise for you are dear to me. Abandon all supports and look to me for protection. I shall purify you from the sins of the past. Do not grieve.

-Krishna in "The Bhagavad Gita"

Shraddha is a remarkable Sanskrit term. There is not an exact translation for the word in English. The term that comes the closest is faith. The literal translation for shraddha is "that which is placed in the heart."

I first learned the term word from my Guru. It is a very rare experience to come into personal contact with a divine mystic. Over the course of one of his dissertations, Yogi Ji taught me of the importance of shraddha. It is an unconditional devotion. I found when I encountered someone who was a pure, unadulterated personification of truth, it felt entirely natural devoting myself unconditionally to internalizing his teachings. A mystic has climbed such an incredibly steep mountain and made a home on the peak of truth and wisdom. There is no undertaking more noble than to dedicate yourself unconditionally to the teachings of an enlightened master so that you may come to an understanding of the truth. If you are so lucky to meet such a person in this life seize the opportunity. Do not take one moment of the experience for granted. You will know in your heart when you have been blessed to meet such a being.

There is no sweeter nectar than to drink from the cup of Shraddha. To devote yourself to a Guru may be even better than to be the Guru himself. If the Guru is the magnet, you are the alloy gravitating toward him or her. When you cease combating the divine current, you learn to effortlessly flow with the energy of the universe.

Yogi Ji guided me to read "The Bhagavad Gita" to develop my knowledge of Shraddha and cultivate an understanding of truth. We become what we hold in our minds. We come to embody the point of our focus. So be discerning of the direction to which you aim your consciousness.

In the Gita, Krishna refers to Shraddha in terms of the gunas (qualities of nature). He describes three levels of faith, sattvic (pure), rajasic (impure), and tamasic (harmful). Krishna describe shraddha in this passage from Chapter 17: 2-3 (Easwaran, Essence of the Bhagavad Gita, 2011).

Every creature is born with faith of some kind either sattvic, rajasic, or tamasic…. Our faith conforms to our nature. Human nature is made of faith. A person is what his shraddha is.

The law of attraction states: you create what you believe. If you think you are human, you will be. When you realize you are divine you will come to embody that truth.

The point of the focus of our faith determines the quality of our existence. An example of tamasic (harmful) shraddha would be to place your faith in the principle of survival of the fittest. This level of understanding leads you to believe it is a dog eat dog world and you must devour competition to get ahead. "By any means necessary" is the mantra for this way of thinking.

Rajasic (impure) shraddha can be exemplified by believing one will find happiness through chasing after desires. The mantra for this way of thinking would be "I just need to make more money and I will be happy."

A sattvic (pure) shraddha is learning to have faith in the divine, living with the understanding that God is guiding you in every aspect of your existence. The mantra for this way of life would be "The divine provides abundance in every aspect of existence". If we create what we believe, the greatest satisfaction will be attained from maintaining pure unconditional devotion (sattvic shraddha) to the divine. Keep God close in your heart so that you may manifest all the divine has in store for you.

In the Ramayana, Hanuman, the ultimate devotee, demonstrates the purest quality of shraddha with the most remarkable devotion. At the end of the Ramayana, Rama (representing God) gives Hanuman a ring as a sign of gratitude for his unwavering devotion. After Rama's departure, Hanuman closely examines the ring, even bites it. He finally throws the ring back into the sea. An onlooker gazes upon Hanuman in disgust and says, "How can you claim to be so devoted to Ram and throw his ring away like that?" Hanuman replied, "I looked all over the ring for Ram's name, even bit it to see if his name was inside, but it was not there, so I discarded the ring." The onlooker said, "You stupid monkey, that was His ring." Hanuman became enraged. In a gory scene of infinite yet gruesome devotion, Hanuman digs his fingernails in his chest. Blood spurts everywhere. As Hanuman opens his chest, Rama and Sita (Ram's wife) are found residing in his heart. Hanuman says, "I do not need a ring to remind me of my Rama because he lives eternally in my heart."

This is true devotion, complete and total shraddha. When realizing God becomes the focus of life, the heart merges in union with the divine. You become the point of your focus and come to embody the object of your devotion. When you hold God near to your heart, you make a home for Him so that He may abide there eternally.

Most people in our society today can only relate to such shraddha through the unhealthy devotion to materialism. The process of transformation takes place as follows: harm (tamas) is transformed to desire (rajas), which is guided toward purity (sattva). Change will take place in our society as materialism is transformed to a desire for *real* happiness. This genuine desire guides us toward an understanding of the interconnectedness of all beings. As you learn to constantly maintain the intense desire to serve God, self-realization is as inevitable as the sunrise after a dark night.

Ascendance

Humankind is on a collective journey. No matter what existential theory you believe, all hypotheses agree that we came from a lower level of consciousness, which suggests we are in route to a higher consciousness.

The three traditionally recognized concepts our society accepts regarding our existence are creation, evolution, and reincarnation. Let's start with creation. This has the least amount of scientific evidence. About our creation, God made the world in seven days. Each day he created beings of higher levels of consciousness. First the world, then small creatures, the reptiles, next winged creatures, mammals, and finally humans, and then he rested on the seventh day. This notion suggests the first forms of consciousness were smaller less intelligent animals. Then God created animals with larger brains and finally humans, who have the greatest level of discernment, intelligence, and consciousness.

In the evolutionary model, animals start as lesser developed creatures with lower levels of intelligence. As the need for more complex development becomes required by the creature's external environment, it physically evolves into a more complex form. In this theory, first physical evolution occurs, then consciousness evolves. But still in evolution, animals and humans come from lesser developed forms. So, what is to say we are done developing as a species?

In reincarnation, conscious beings evolve to higher or lower level life forms based on their accumulated karma from life to life. Lower level forms are rocks and plants, then smaller to larger animals and finally humankind. Eventually, when an individual soul wins the game of karma (which is won by not playing the game at all) it has no need for a physical body and merges with the creator ending the cycle of reincarnation. The difference between reincarnation and evolution is that in reincarnation the consciousness evolves first and the development of the physical form follows.

What all these theories have in common is they agree we are not done developing physically, mentally, or spiritually. All major religions have stories of flesh and blood beings reaching some sort of enlightened state or spiritual perfection and ascending the human body. Take for instance the story of Jesus in Christianity, Elijah in Judaism, Buddha in Buddhism, Mohammed in Islam, and several individuals in the Hindu tradition all ascended the physical body and merged with the divine. No matter your religious belief or to what existential theory you subscribe, they are all in basic agreement. The journey of consciousness takes a lesser-developed being through numerous stages of progression until transcending the physical body and merging with the divine universal consciousness.

Now you might be asking yourself if this can really all be true and if so how is it possible? A few years ago a fad was trending among Christians. Everyone was wearing bracelets that read the acronym WWJD. This stood for "What Would Jesus Do". It is really a great concept to keep people conscious about the intention behind individual actions. I asked myself "what was Jesus doing?" He was preparing himself for ascension, to evolve past the need for a physical body and merge in unison with the divine heavenly Father. How did he accomplish this? By following the path of Buddha and realizing that all life is suffering. Suffering is designed to push us along in our spiritual evolution. The sooner you realize suffering is a blessing from God the sooner you will take your next evolutionary step forward.

Nothing ever changes when the circumstances are comfortable. Does the business world ever change in an upward trending market? No! Change comes about in hard times. Animals do not physically evolve because they are comfortable. They evolve when they are starving to death and their habitat is quickly changing. The suffering we experience is the design of the universal order. Suffering encourages us to step out of our comfort zone, to leave the small birdcage view of the world and spread our wings. Without suffering there would be no change, no growth. How did Jesus harness the painful power of his suffering and transform it into growth? Through meditation he could detach from the conditioning behind his mental process. Why do you meditate? Meditation is food for the soul. When you withdraw your senses from the physical world and focus inward, you begin your work on a higher, subtler realm of existence. This reality is accessed through prayer, meditation, or other form of spiritual practice. Modern culture does all it can to hold us back from evolving by stimulating our external senses through TV, music, video games, electronics, consumerism, materialism and all sorts of other isms. I am not saying these things are inherently bad, but unless you know how to traverse this world with consciousness, your physical senses will only hold you back in your journey. Through meditation, you learn to heighten your vibrations of consciousness, which makes you more aware of what is happening in all realms.

There comes a point when the physical body is no longer needed to continue your work. It is possible to ascend to this level yet remain in the human body and guide others forward. We are all in it together. Consciousness is a universal movement. Through meditation, you come to higher understandings of values like truth, humility, honesty, and service. The sooner all people realize we are here to serve the world, the sooner we will begin to live in harmony with the planet and in service to our fellow man or woman. The world needs balance. The sooner we find that balance the sooner the planetary consciousness develops into a new stage of evolution.

Part 2:

Applying the Wisdom of Patanjali and the Yogic Tradition

When you are inspired by some great purpose, some extraordinary project, all your thoughts break their bonds; your mind transcends limitations, your consciousness expands in every direction, and you find yourself in a new, great, and wonderful world. Dormant forces, faculties and talents become alive, and you discover yourself to be a greater person by far than you ever dreamed yourself to be.

-Patanjali

Chapter 9: Introducing the Yoga Sutras

The First Sutra

Atha Yoganushasam
Now the teachings of Yoga

The first word in this sutra is "atha," which means now. This use of the word now cues us for what is ahead and encourages the reader to come to attention and prepare to receive this ancient wisdom teaching. The word now is meant to wake the reader from a slumber in the night of ignorance and to be ready to see the light clearly in this new day of knowledge. "Yoganushasam" is a very long word that essential describes an understanding of the practice of yoga. Although short and very concise, this sutra is heavy and holds much gravity. So, I, too, encourage you, sit up straight, make haste and ready yourself for the magnificent teachings of yoga as taught by Patanjali.

The word sutra refers to a thread interweaving the tapestry of all the sacred teachings of the ancient teachers in the yogic traditions. A sutra is a short phrase with a tremendous meaning. The Yoga Sutras are a radical pioneering work for anyone studying spirituality. Patanjali left us a roadmap to complete the next step in the evolution of the spirit. The sutras describe a step-by-step scientific process that gives the spiritual aspirant a clear path and a decisive method to achieve the objective of all spiritual disciplines. The sutras demystify the esoteric teachings of the ancients. With dedicated effort, a seeker can utilize the wisdom of the sutras to accomplish his or her purpose in life.

An entire chapter could easily be written describing each sutra. In this section of the book I will briefly describe the first three sutras and cover several of the other important elements of Patanjali's teachings. There are four chapters in the Yoga Sutras. The first explains what yoga is. The second chapter explains how to do yoga. The third chapter covers the special powers attained through yoga. The fourth chapter defines what enlightenment is. I encourage you to study Patanjali's sutras in their entirety if you are interested in this subject matter. What is covered in this book is meant as an introduction and very brief overview to the teachings of Patanjali. There is a vast amount of literature covering the Sutras in their full depth. Please see the work cited pages for some books I recommend on the subject.

The Second Sutra

Yoga Citta Vritta Nirodaha

Yoga is the Cessation of the fluctuations of the mind

In the second sutra, we are given the first immense teaching of Patanjali. In very short clear understandable language Patanjali explains concisely what is yoga. First, he gives us the word "yoga". The word yoga means to yoke, like the tying together of something. Union is also often used to describe the word yoga. The three elements of life that are united by the yoga practice are the mind, body, and spirit. The union of mind, body and spirit is a reference to enlightenment. A yogi, or individual who has attained the goal of yoga, is an enlightened being. "Citta" is the mind-body connection. "Vritta" refers to a mental fluctuation. "Nirodaha" is the ending or cessation of a process. So basically, Patanjali is saying, enlightenment is when thoughts cease and the mind becomes still. The yogi ends the false identification with thoughts and sees himself and the world for what it truly is.

Our emotions truly affect the happiness and quality of life we experience on a momentary basis. What are emotions? Emotions are a physical reaction in the body to the thought process. Like waves in the ocean, our emotions are constantly in a fluid state. Waves naturally rise and fall; like our emotions and our thoughts. The important technique here is to understand and disconnect from life's fluctuations. Waves continuously rise and fall. Emotions go up, down, then up again, and back down again. The process is continuous and never ending. When you can take the seat of the witness, you begin to see the movement in your own emotions without being attached to them. When you come to understand the pattern, you gain the insight to see the future. Happiness is followed by sadness, followed by happiness, which in turn is followed by sadness. From the eye of the witness, you realize you are not your emotions.

Emotions are merely a product of your mind, but they are not you. You are the driver; the mind is the GPS in your vehicle. The mind is a storage device for information that we use to make decisions while navigating our chosen course. But just like the GPS, you do not always take the mind's advice. Your GPS is not intuitive, just like the mind. Intuition comes from somewhere else. Somewhere close to your core. Following the GPS blindly often takes you off course and can prolong your journey.

The emotions are often compared to water. For instance, the water signs used in astrology are considered the most emotional signs, like Cancer, Pisces, and Aquarius. Emotions go up and down like waves. Know that when you are sad, it will not last forever. The emotion will be followed by happiness. When you are happy, appreciate the moment for its impermanence. Following Patanjali's advice in the second sutra, if you pull back in the moment you are feeling happiness, the wave will not grow so high and the crashing of sadness will not fall so low. To really end the fluctuations of the mind do not try to control anything. Disassociate from the fluctuations. Realize you are not your emotions. You will come to enjoy the dance of life through the eyes of witness. It will be like you are in the audience appreciating the show. You can watch the play of existence unfold in front of your eyes. You are not the play but the one watching the play.

Watching others go through emotional fluctuations, you can experience their drama and remain emotionally detached. Relationships are a great example of the roller coaster of emotions. People get so attached in relationships that they often have a difficult time letting go even when the end is inevitable. These people need guidance from their friends and teachers because their emotional attachment prevents them from thinking intelligently. We have both an IQ (intellectual intelligence) and an EQ (emotional intelligence). Always in life, the healthiest path is through the middle road. A balance between IQ and EQ is necessary to thrive in life. Maintaining the equilibrium between the head and the heart, the masculine and feminine allows one to achieve the totality of their potential. Realizing the play of the emotional melodrama in the lives of others helps us to heighten our own emotional awareness.

Riding emotional waves makes for a turbulent life. Learn to detach from your emotions. This does not mean you do not care about life, but you are detached from the outcomes of your actions and the instability associated with emotional fluctuation. Operate from a sense of righteousness and then the results are less important. Accept others for who they are and allow them to make their own decisions. In detachment, we overcome the need to judge others or ourselves. Love yourself and others for who they really are, not for their actions or the results of their actions. Do not waste energy on judgment and you will maintain a more balanced equilibrium.

Becoming the witness of the mind frees you from the current of emotional tides and allows you to submerse yourself in the sea of compassion. These vibrations operate at a much deeper plane of existence. When you dive deep in the ocean, the water is peaceful and does not fluctuate. When you stop the fluctuations, you achieve union with the divine. You cease living in duality and become a drop of water in the ocean of love. Giving up the false sense of control allows you to merge into the reality of bliss.

The Ring

Once upon a time a king made a special ring. He wanted to put a special, meaningful inscription inside the ring. He sought out a wise yogi who lived in the forest and asked the yogi for a message he could inscribe in the ring. The yogi agreed to give him a powerful mantra, but told the king not to look at the words on the ring unless he was in a moment of crisis or mortal danger.

Years passed and the king's empire flourished. One day, completely out of the blue, a large army attacked and invaded the kingdom. Entirely unprepared for the invasion, the kingdom was overwhelmed. The city walls were quickly breeched and nearly all the defending soldiers were killed. Even the king's personal guards were all killed.

Somehow the king narrowly escaped with his life. He rode on horseback into the wilderness with the best soldiers of the invading army in close pursuit. The king's horse became winded and then he was forced to flee on foot. Coming to a cliff, the king's only option was to hide. He was sure the end of his life was nearing impending doom when he remembered the ring. Clearly, this was a moment of mortal danger. The king took off his ring and read the wise man's special message inscribed inside. It read, "This too shall pass."

He took a deep breath and realized the impermanence inherent to all emotions. Finding peace within himself, the king remained hidden behind in a thicket of shrubbery. The enemy soldiers looked but could not find the king. Eventually, the soldiers gave up and returned to their newly gained territory.

Surviving with his life, the king came out of hiding. He went to a small village on the outskirts of what remained of his kingdom and began to amass an army. After one year, the king's army was large enough to attack and regain his entire kingdom.

All emotions are impermanent. They are only temporary creations of the mind. Retaking control of our destiny, we come to the objective understanding that emotions are momentary and will soon change. This allows you to remain conscious of the big picture. Sometimes it is good to wait; other times action is required. Some situations are in your face and require immediate attention. Others permit time for contemplation. It is always best to maintain a clear perception of reality so that you can use your ability to discern the correct action. Do not act on emotion, live with understanding. Choose to respond instead of react.

The Third Sutra

Tadah Swarupe Avastanam

The Seer stands revealed in its true form

When you end the fluctuations of the mind and revel in total awe of the stillness encompassing your consciousness there is an incredible realization. You are not your mind or your thoughts. Your viewpoint is from a place of witnessing thought. What or who is that? You can spend many lifetimes meditating this question. Patanjali tells us, you are the seer. You are the one who sees thought from the perspective of source. I hesitate to place a specific name or title on source as all traditions have a different designation for this term. Some call it God, Higher Power, Universal Order, or Jesus Christ. There are many labels for the source energy powering the universe, but only one truth. You are that truth. Christ taught, "I am the way, the truth, and the light." At your source, you are all this and more than can ever possibly be described by mere words alone. At your essential core, you are source. The source energy encompassing your spirit is the underlying connection uniting all things.

When we were in the womb, only oneness existed. We did not even have a concept of separation. We were in direct connection with our life force. At the moment we were born, the umbilical cord was cut and the illusion of separation began.

Nature automatically drops this thin veil at birth. Society quickly constructs a wall that reinforces the belief of separation.

As babies, we felt separate when we came to know hunger. Crying from suffering, our mother reunites us with the divine milk that nourishes the idea of unity. As we became toddlers, we learned the idea of "me", "mine", and "I". "These are my toys", and "That is my food". These beliefs reinforce the idea of separation that "these material things belong only to me" and "I am different than you".

As we grow, our capitalist society reinforces the illusionary wall with bricks of materialism. I need these clothes, this car, this house, this life. The only real reason we feel we need things is to live up to our concept of the personality we have artificially created. When we were born, our personality was created and we were given a name. Do not let your name be just another ego complex. Make your name represent and expression of the divine, a realization of God.

Others will attempt to encourage you to sculpt your idea of your own personality by saying things like, "You are so handsome", "She is so slender", or "He is so talented". These qualities are all descriptions inflate the ego that keeps us separated from oneness. The search should really be oriented toward connecting with your authentic self.

Our personality keeps us separated from the source. The search for our true identity guides us toward the authentic self, toward oneness. Learning to identify with the divine is the ultimate aspiration. Personality is unreal, borrowed from others' perception of us. We are innately born questioning, "Why am I here?" In separation, you cannot realize your purpose. Through meditation, we focus awareness inward past all the layers of conditioning to our authentic self. Letting go of each image you create of yourself, you take down a brick from the wall separating you from your Self. One day you will notice a subtle change in yourself. The wall will have vanished completely. It will disappear when you, like a turtle withdrawing into its shell, withdraw from the world of sensory stimulation and become established in the inner realm of the spirit. This is the tearing of the veil separating you from your truth. You will have achieved union with the divine, self-realization. You come to understand we are not separate at all but one single entity functioning in unison.

The body is made of organs that are made of cells made of molecules, made of atoms, made of light, made of vibrations. You, me and the space between us exist of entirely of energy vibrations. We are all one. You are not a separate, isolated, individual entity. Every single human being is a materialization of divinity with a specific individual purpose. Realize your purpose, connect with God and masterfully enact your roll in the cosmic play of the divine.

The fact the ego can never be happy proves the existence of the divine. The ego cannot be happy because its will can never be realized and this will is separate from the divine will. The authentic self exists in the realm of sheer happiness. It also explains our current collective state of separation. God's will always manifest despite all distortive attempts of the ego. You will know peace when you surrender to the divine will and connect to your innate oneness.

Chapter 10: Basics Concepts of Yoga Philosophy

Layers of the Self

A beautiful concept described in the Taittiriya Upanishad (one of the most ancient Hindu scriptures) delineating the aspects of the self is the model of the koshas. A kosha is a sheath or covering of the Highest Self. Like layers of the onion, the philosophy of the koshas scientifically explains the layers of the self from gross to subtle, from physical to metaphysical. Another metaphor that can be used to understand the makeup of the koshas is that of the little Russian dolls. A small wooden doll when opened holds another doll. Opening that doll uncovers another layer and yet another. Embarking on our spiritual journey takes us from our grossest form, the physical body, to the subtlest aspect of the self, the soul.

There are five layers of the self: the anamaya kosha (the physical body), the pranamaya kosha (the breath body), the manomaya kosha (the mental body), the vijanmaya kosha (the intellectual body), and the anandamaya kosha (the bliss body). Through the practice of yoga and meditation, we realize the existence of a conditioned identification with the physical body. In this primary realization, we discover we are much more than a mere physical form and embark on a journey of the path to discovery of the true self.

The Anamaya Kosha (The Physical Body)

The physical body is only one aspect of the self. Our body is the most impermanent part of ourselves. We have two sets of senses: external and internal. Modern society is entirely extroverted and oriented toward the outer world. Entertainment forms such as television, music, video, food, alcohol, sex are all forms of external sensory stimulation. Open any magazine and you will see numerous ads focusing the identification with the physical body. Nearly everything we do in our modern culture focuses awareness on the most external layer of being. I am not saying food, music, television, and sex are bad, instead merely recognize they are forms of external sensory stimulation. Meditation, yoga, deep breathing techniques, and practicing silence are methods of internal sensory stimulation designed and performed to focus attention inward. To know the truth, to know yourself, your focus must be directed inward.

Identification with the physical body prevents the realization of the authentic self and all we are truly meant to be. The physical self is only one part of our whole being. Most see themselves as only what is tangible in the physical realm. You are much, much more than just your body. The anamaya kosha is the grossest layer in a metaphysical system that progresses subtly. Directing focus from the outside in is the first step in the process of realization the totality of the true self.

The Pranamaya Kosha (The Breath Body)

To begin our transformation, we must shed the first most external layer. The process begins as we deepen our awareness from our body to our breathing. Therefore, most forms of meditation and all forms of yoga focus so intensely on the quality of the breath. Most spiritual disciplines I am aware of begin by tuning into the sensation of breathing.

Focusing awareness on the breath shifts our attention to the next subtler layer of the metaphysical body, the pranamaya kosha. The word "Prana" is more than just the breath. It is synonymous with "chi" from Tai chi, or "qi" from qigong. Western religions term this energy as spirit. Prana is accurately translated as life force. The four basic elements of survival are shelter, food, water, and air. We can technically survive without shelter. The physical body cannot go much longer than a few weeks without food. The human body cannot go longer that a few days without water. The body cannot survive more than a matter of minutes without air. Therefore, breath is the most essential element to survival. In terms of metaphysical anatomy, the breath represents the flow or movement of source energy through the body.

Paying attention to the breath can teach us much about our state of being. If breathing is short and unsteady, one is likely nervous and ungrounded. When the breath is full and steady, the tendency is to be calm and grounded emotionally.

When you take a deep breath, you trigger the vagus nerve sending a chemical signaling relaxation to the brain and triggering the parasympathetic nervous system into operation. This is why my mother told me when acting out as a hyperactive child to take a deep breath and count to 10. Connecting to the breath body is a powerful way to find your center at any moment. To check into the pranamaya kosha all you need do is tune your awareness to the rise and fall of the breath.

Manomaya Kosha (The Mental Body)

Peeling back one more layer of the onion, we have the mind body, the manomaya kosha. Once you become established in the breath body through the help of some breathing or meditation practice, all sorts of thoughts begin to arise in your consciousness. As soon as you settle into a meditation practice, thoughts start appearing in your mind. You cannot control these thoughts. The method to disassociate with these thoughts is to associate your real self as the witness of these thoughts. As the witness, you become aware of different aspects of your mental process (such as emotions or ego) and understand where your thoughts are coming from.

Through sadhana (spiritual practice), a depth of understanding of the manomaya kosha develops. An analogy to describe the manomaya kosha is an egg with three elements: the shell, the ovum, and the yoke.

The Shell

The shell represents the conditioned mind. This is an ingrained way of thinking created from a lifetime of discontent, always wanting more, and searching for happiness from outside. Conditioning started the moment we were born and began living in the illusion of duality, recognizing ourselves as separate from all other life. In the shell, we trained ourselves to live instinctually like animals operating unconsciously and reactively from past experiences without discernment. Getting upset, using the horn on the freeway, smoking cigarettes one after another every moment stress presents itself, and getting defensive every time a friend uses constructive criticism are all examples of operating out of habit instead of using discernment.

The Ovum

Becoming the witness to our thoughts, we gain the ability to differentiate the shell from the ovum. In this analogy, the ovum represents the ego, the source of misperception and cause behind identification with the emotions.

In the shell, we identify with our secondary emotions such as anger, hatred, and frustration. These are reactionary emotions based on experiences outside of ourselves created by the ego. In meditation, we get an opportunity to take a closer look at the ego and realize it creates all emotions. The ego creates a secondary emotion to avoid dealing with primary emotions. For instance, anger comes from an aversion to feeling shame of a childhood failure.

In high school, I felt a great deal of pressure placed on me by my family to excel academically. To avoid feeling shame from not meeting their and my own unrealistic expectations, I focused on ager toward others, which ultimately led to drug use. I created a habitual way of escaping my emotions. Anger was the secondary emotion; shame was the primary emotion. To avoid the feeling the pain of identifying with shame, I found a way to escape it. I turned to anger to shift my focus outside of myself at others. In the great discomfort of my anger, I used drugs to escape the pain. Getting to the yolk of the egg is the way to finally understand and overcome the problem.

The Yolk

Continuing the analogy, we have made it to the yolk, the essence of who we truly are. The true self is beyond the ego and has an understanding and disassociation from the emotional self.

Your mind is only a part of you. At your core, your true self, you are not your mind. The brain is an organ. You can become conscious of the workings of the brain like you become conscious of your heart beating. But the mind has a different function than the heart. The heart circulates blood, the brain circles in thought. We must be discerning of our mind. You must learn to use the brain more like a muscle than an organ. You tell the brain when to think and what to think. You are the master of your brain; it is not the master of you. With discernment, you decide to act or to feel using discretion based on the multitude of thoughts coming from mind.

You do not have to listen or identify with your thoughts when you develop the ability to operate in awareness. There is always a different way to look at things. Life can be seen as a glass half full or half empty. You can live in misery or in gratitude, you decide. At first awareness is fleeting, but over time, as a result of consistent practice, the ability to be constantly aware of thought develops.

The Vijanmaya Kosha (Intellect Body)

      The next layer of self we pass through on our journey is the vijanmaya kosha or the intellect body. Very few make it to this layer of self for any prolonged period of time. Great thinkers like Einstein, Tesla, Tolstoy, and poets like Rumi, and Hafiz were well acquainted in the intellectual body. Intellect gains much of its ability by passing beyond the spaced clouded by the ego. The way we judge keeps us from realizing our intellectual potential. Judging and blaming keep us from delving further into unlimited creative thought. This is a place where the impossible can be achieved. When we stop judging ourselves, others, and situations, the separation between the individual microcosm from the interconnected macrocosm

begin to disintegrate. This sense of clarity gives one the opportunity to be insightful to a degree previously unknown. Those who are firmly established in the vijanmaya kosha are perfectly comfortable spending time alone. This time allows opportunity for deep contemplation and meditation on the unfathomable questions of life. An advanced understanding and creativity in utilizing mathematics, science, and literature become more accessible as our level of connectedness to whole broadens.

      Being unattached to the fruits of his or her labor allows the individual established in the vijanmaya kosha to continue their search for wisdom to a degree further than others who operate from a place of goal-centered attachment. Knowledge is factual intelligence. Wisdom is the understanding and implementation of universal truth. The realm of the wise is a place where the aesthetic and the scientific find union. The flow of the divine intellectual current clarifies as we begin to see ourselves as a single entity of a much greater whole.

Anandamaya Kosha (Bliss Body)

Once I laid on the beach in La Jolla. It was a beautiful sunny day. I had just finished practicing yoga asana with my beloved teacher. Body and breath were in tune; my mind was still. At the spur of the moment, the opportunity for meditation presented itself. I closed my eyes and focused my awareness on my breath. The temperature was perfect as the sun shone on my body. I could hear the waves crashing and receding. It felt as if the movement of the ocean was the planet's process of inspiration and expiration. My breath and the planet's breath became one. I felt my body temperature cool and was intuitively aware of a cloud passing between the sun and myself. The momentary experience passed as the sun enlightened my body again. I could feel the mist of the ocean gently cover me and quickly evaporate as the surf crashed against the rocks. My body, mind, and soul aligned creating a union with all of existence. Bliss permeated every cell of my being.

The further we travel on our journey to the soul the less we will be able to describe our experience with any language. Words do not begin to come close to possessing the ability to describe the experience of knowing bliss. In the anandamaya kosha, you will recognize synchronicity, know the purpose, and understand the unity between all things. The experience of ishvara pranidhana (surrendering to the divine will) permeates from the essence of being throughout every layer. The need for hope leaves your psyche. One hope realized creates 100 hopes to be crushed. We hope for things when we separate our will from God's. When your will merges with the divine's, you find peace. The ability of your intuition increases tremendously. Your internal light begins to glow externally.

The Five Lenses

A telescope has multiple lenses to extend the range of its function. With one lens, a telescope can see no more than a few hundred yards. Utilizing five lenses, perhaps it could see hundreds or even thousands of miles away.

Each kosha, or layer of self, operates like a lens within the telescope. Through the scope of any single lens, or kosha, we only see life through one aspect of the self. Seeing ourselves through all five levels of self dramatically increases our perspective of the world.

At different times in your life you may have had experiences in any or all the koshas. While shopping for clothes we see ourselves in the anamaya kosha, the physical self. Practicing yoga asana, we connect to the breath body. During an emotional time at work we orient toward the mind body. Writing a very technical paper for a college class perhaps we experience the intellectual body most clearly. During a religious service, you can experience the bliss body.

At certain times in our lives any layer could be functioning more clearly than the rest. Let's say all levels of the self are clear except the emotional body due to problems in a relationship. This would be analogous to one lens in the telescope being smudged or clouded. One unclear layer prevents the whole from operating in unison. When we clear all layers of self, the light of awareness can shine clearly from the inside out. The true self can manifest through every layer of reality and transparently illuminate the material world. By mastering the three methods of Kriya yoga, daily practice, selfstudy, and surrender to the divine will, the lenses of perception are polished.

The Three Elements of Nature

There are three elements of nature that can be used to understand the quality in all things from the food we eat to the type of thoughts we have. The three gunas (elements) are: sattva, rajas, and tamas. Like an existential rope, the qualities of nature tie all things together. The gunas are commonly used to describe the physical characteristics of things. Our understanding becomes more meaningful when we use the gunas to describe internal characteristics like our emotional state.

Sattva is used to describe that which is most pure in nature. Ideas such as love, purity, harmony, compassion, and selfless service are all examples of ideals that are sattvic. Rajas can be used to describe that which is harmful to the self. Qualities like attachment, desire, and sorrow all represent the rajasic state. Tamas is that which is harmful to others. Dullness, heaviness, darkness, and illusion describe the tamasic state.

No single guna is ever a permanent fixation in life. These elements tend to circle each other as individual strands that form a rope tying reality together. Like a wave has highs and lows the gunas are in a state of constant flux in life. If a person began in a tamasic state there would be qualities like heaviness, ill health, and stagnation. As he or she began to improve the self, there would be a transition into a state of rajas, becoming more active. Burning off impurities requires effort. Eventually one comes to the graceful state of complete purity, sattva. The reality is this state cannot be maintained indefinitely. Nothing in the material world is permanent. In an effort to maintain sattva, we expend much energy becoming rajastic. Once we exhaust ourselves by expending the energy required to maintain rajas, tamasic and we become lazy. These qualities are in constant motion. With awareness, we can bring our attention to our current state, how we got there, and the method to maintaining or improving that state.

There is a wonderful book named "Peaks and Valleys" by Spencer Johnson. The book describes our natural state of fluctuation in life through a short story. The tale is about a man who hikes up a mountain to meet a wise teacher on the peak. Every time he makes it to the peak, life is blissful, but eventually the young man must return to the valley to recuperate and is filled with longing for the peak. During the story the young man matures and realizes what he can do while he is in the valley to get out of that place (or emotional state) faster. He must expend great energy to hike to the peak. When he is on the peak he becomes aware of what he can do while he is in the valley to stay on the peak for longer durations of time. This story illustrates the transition of the gunas in life.

The Permanent and Impermanent

Yogic philosophy describes two realities of existence as principles known as prakriti (permanent) and purusha (impermanent). Prakriti is the external world of nature, the territory of impermanence. Purusha is the internal world, the realm of permanence, and the soul. Meditate on what in life is permanent or impermanent.

A rock does not change much over the course of the time since its creation one million years ago. What will happen to that rock one million years from now? Something more impermanent than a rock is a car you buy new from the dealership. In our society, after five years the car will go through some wear and tear becoming less desirable than a new car. That new car smell will be long gone. After 10 years, the car is nearly obsolete and entirely socially undesirable. Its paint is wearing and the vehicle will be fast approaching the maximum number of miles it was designed for. Fifty years later, the vehicle will no longer exist. Hopefully, it was recycled and used to make another vehicle. If left to the elements, the fluctuations of the impermanent seasons in nature will all but erode the vehicle back to nothingness.

Does your higher power or your soul ever change? Meditate deeply on this. God and the soul do not change as they exist in the dominion of the eternal (purusha), the inner world of the infinite. What changes in our relationship with the divine is our perception of the soul and our relationship to God. As our perception falls under the guise of impermanence (prakriti), it is ever changing. A spiritual aspirant's perception is clarified through spiritual practice. With an illuminated perspective, the understanding of God transforms, improving the quality of the relationship. Eventually we make the ultimate realization of union with the divine, removing all barriers of separation, merging into oneness with truth.

Consciousness and Awareness

Consciousness and awareness exist as two very different perspectives of reality. It is easy to settle with the thought that the meaning of these words as the same. Allow me to clarify. Consciousness is active in nature (prakriti). Awareness encompasses conscious in the realm of the timeless and eternal (purusha).

In meditative philosophy, the idea of the object and the subject is often used. As an example, I will use the act of watching television. The object is the television displaying its image. You represent the subject viewing the object of the television. The action of watching the television is your consciousness in play. You are consciously watching the television. Awareness is the experience encompassing this entire scene. It is the point of view aware of the entire scene of you consciously watching the television from an objective point of view.

In the realm of nature, consciousness is ruled by emotion. Awareness is beyond the fluctuations of emotions viewing existence without the bias, constraints, or any attachments to time. Everyone has the capacity to be cognizant of both consciousness and awareness.

The act of being present in the moment allows an individual to directly experience his or her consciousness firsthand. The process of meditation allows the practitioner to access the eternal, non-judgmental realm of awareness. Describing awareness can be little more than a paradoxical effort. Words are limited by their meaning. The power of pure awareness is unlimited and unmanifested in every aspect. Awareness exists as all things. It is impossible to define the infinite in a manifested reality with a wordy description bound by limitation. This is precisely why spiritual teachers of every age encourage the aspirant to delve deeply inward to experience the Eternal personally. This is the only way to truly know. In the depth of the ocean of the self exists the portal unlocking access to the realization of the Universal Self.

Hazrat Inayat Khan's statement is appropriate here, "It is not by self-realization that man realizes God, it is by God realization that man realizes self." It could be argued that the unmanifest God is itself awareness. During the meditation practice thoughts instantaneously arise. When the aspirant focuses attention he or she can observe the thought process with attachment from a place of pure awareness. *The willingness to observe thoughts and experiences without reaction facilitates an effortless meditation guiding one toward the mastery of life.* Attachment creates reactions, judgments and blame separating the individual from the entirety of humanity. The understanding actualized by acceptance overcomes separation and takes you deeper down the path of realization.

The introductory state of awareness can be likened to watching a storm. A large cloud thunders and the noise of the rain is heard in every direction. As the quality of awareness heightens, you can differentiate between the sounds of the thunder, the rain, and the wind all made by the storm. At the highest level of awareness, you notice individual raindrops falling. You recognize the temperature, and the smell of the rain. You even anticipate the smell of the ozone that will permeate the air after the storm passes. Awareness is even beyond the constraints of time.

Once you have accumulated some experience with your chosen meditation technique, try meditating in a public area where noise will be inevitable. Do not judge sounds or the people or things making the sounds. Simply allow yourself to experience the moment in total awareness. You see you are surrounded by individual flickers of light or energy all creating one magnificent reality entirely dependent on every single participant. A sense of gratitude, reverence, and awe will permeate every layer of your being as you enjoy experiencing the interplay of reality all around you from the perspective of pure awareness. Soak it all in like earth soaks up the storm. You are the earth and the storm is the movement of consciousness all around you.

Permanence, Impermanence, and the Gunas in Practice

Looking at some aspects of the self through the models of prakriti and purusha, and the qualities of nature we will cover one aspect of this topic in terms of diet. Food choices serve as a great example. When the seed of awareness is planted, we likely have developed little if any consciousness about the importance of healthy eating. This transitory period represents a state of tamas (harm). Overeating, consuming too much food makes us feel lazy. Eating lots of meat, which is harmful to others, has many detrimental effects on our health. As our awareness grows, we cut out the red meat, but still eat fried and processed food. We have more energy because we are not slowed down by the red meat in our diet. There is still room for improvement as processed food is not the best for our health. As awareness heightens to new levels, we start eating more raw food, organic fruits and vegetables. Our diet has become cleaner and purer. We notice the change. Our body has much more energy, lightness, and functions with an efficiency never known before.

As all things in nature are impermanent we likely do not maintain such a pristine diet interminably. We do not yet know enough to maintain a sattvic state indefinitely. Perhaps we have not supplemented the absence of meat in our diet with an adequate amount of protein. In a quest for energy, we start drinking three or four cups of coffee a day becoming more rajasic. Eventually, we start eating more food frantically to fuel the increased energy output. With the ebb and flow of our awareness, the quality of our diet rises and falls. When we develop enough awareness in our diet to become primarily sattvic regarding diet our habits habit become more than a routine. Making eating choices consciously has become a lifestyle instead of a short-term diet. There will still be small fluctuations in the lifestyle. Maybe eating too many sweets on occasion or not drinking enough water will cause the stability of diet to vacillate. Nature is in constant movement. The absence of fluctuation would mean the absence of life.

Like the chemical states of gas, liquid, and solid, we are always moving, even when we appear not to be. In a gaseous, state molecules move the most. A liquid apparently moves. At the molecular level liquids move at an increased rate with a smaller stride. In a solid object, movement of molecules occurs even faster than in gaseous and liquid states, they just have a smaller pattern of movement. The point I am getting to at is in all states there is movement. The awareness of this movement is what really matters.

The last example I will use to explain the gunas is our thoughts. When we begin our spiritual journey, maybe our thoughts are 99 percent harmful to other (tamas), always acting out in anger. As our consciousness of living in harmony toward others grows, day-by-day we work on the quality of our thoughts, transforming anger. Anger is a secondary emotion. The primary emotions behind anger are usually fear, pain, or shame. Through a great deal of introspection (rajas), we create awareness of our emotions by humbling ourselves and transforming our anger and finally personally admitting our fears. Recall from Chapter 1, fear and love are the same energy moving in the opposite directions. In meditation, one finds the courage to surrender thus transforming the emotion of fear to love.

I will refer to the metaphor of the rope used earlier to describe the transformation of the gunas. Imagine the rope has been made into a whip. When thrown, the whip fluctuates travelling up and down to increase speed. At the end of its journey the whip snaps. The movement of the whip represents the transitions in the gunas. The snap of the whip represents the moment of realization in which we become enlightened. After the snap the whip still moves. The difference now is that we are conscious of the movement and act accordingly. The enlightened mind cannot stop fluctuations in the material world. The best way to change the outer world is to change the inner world. With awareness, we can utilize the philosophy from peaks and valleys maximizing our time in the sattvic state.

Vegetarianism

A proper diet is incredibly important for the spiritual aspirant. Vegetarianism is the traditional diet for the yogic tradition as ahimsa or non-harm to all living creatures is a paramount guideline in the practice. What we put into our body affects us from our grosses to our most subtle self. It is important to keep the gunas in mind and eat in the most sattvic way possible. I am proposing another way to look at our spiritual evolution in terms of diet. Everything has its own karma, even the food we eat. Did the process creating the food we eat involve harming others? Everything, even food we eat is vibration at is most basic. If food was harvested in a harmful manner, it holds that vibration. When we ingest that food, we ingest its vibration and become it. The saying, "You are what you eat" may have more meaning that you ever imagined. When I leaned about "The World Peace Diet" designed by Dr. William Tuttle, I was at first skeptical. I quickly gained a deeper understanding of how what we eat not only affects us but also the world around us. Tuttle suggests that the method in which we create our food adversely affects our karma societally.

A clear and painful example of the collective karma accumulated from the Western diet is the factory production of meat. Please bear with me through the gory details. Factory farmed cows are artificially inseminated on a machine known as a rape rack. The cows experience much pain as a metal device is forcefully interested in their reproductive organs. When the cow gives birth, its calf is immediately taken away from its mother never to see her again. The cow is instantly reinseminated. Throughout the life of the cow it is inject with steroids, hormones, and a host of other pharmaceuticals. The cow is forced to eat food enriched with proteins derived from others cows so it can maintain its proper size. This naturally vegetarian animal is forced to become a cannibal. Naturally producing five gallons of milk a day, these drugged up cows produce more than 120 gallons of milk a day. The cow should live to be nearly 20 years old, but after all the inhumane treatment it experiences because of our factory farming system, it lives to be only three or four years of age before it must be sent to slaughter.

Environmentally this process has a terrible effect on the planet. The cows in the United States produce more greenhouse gases than all our cars combined. When it comes to water, the result is catastrophic. To produce one pound of wheat or tomatoes requires 250 gallons of water. To produce one pound of beef requires 2,500 gallons of water. I end this line of thought here before your eyes jump out of your head. There are enough examples to demonstrate the disastrous environmental effect of meat product that I could write a book about the subject. If you are interested, I encourage you to do your own research.

The karmic result of this system is visibly evident. Keep in mind Albert Einstein (who was also a vegetarian), famously stated, "Every action has an equal and opposite reaction." Cows are forced on a rape rack to be artificially inseminated. On the karmic flip side, rape is a horrible epidemic worldwide to humankind known to take place in nearly every community on the planet. Infertility is also becoming a greater and greater concern on a global scale. Perhaps meat consumption is a source of the problem.

Cows are forced to use a host of drugs to increase production. In our society, the drug war is a losing cause. Communities in all countries experience some degree of illegal drug use that tears families apart. Certain individuals feel they need to use "uppers" to accomplish enough work to be successful in their careers. Could this be a karmic revolution of our societal eating habits?

The way all these sentient beings (referring to cows) are forced into a life of unethical treatment is horrible. In the United States, more people are imprisoned (by percentage and sheer number) than any other society on the history of the planet. The actual number is more than 2 million people! More than 90 percent of those in jail are imprisoned because of drug use. Could this be the karmic backswing of the way we care for the livestock that provide our sustenance?

Greenhouse gases have devastated the planet's atmosphere. The issue has become more and more dire every day. This matter is a direct result of the way our society produces, transports, and consumes food. Another argument that could be made that is even more of a stretch relates to the deaths resulting from the wars in the Middle East and the drug wars in Central and South America are a karmic reaction to the factory production of meat.

The lifespan of cows has dramatically decreased because of the quality of their treatment. The rate of cancer more than doubled in those who eat read meat regularly. If this is not a direct karmic result from consuming animals, I do not know what is.

Stop eating red meat as soon as possible. Eventually stop eating chicken, and when you have gained enough momentum and knowledge about how to eat enough plant protein, cut out fish as well. Vegetarianism or veganism may seem like a huge lifestyle change, but the world needs incredible change. We must get past our societal conditioning to realize how to truly live in harmony with the planet. People say, "I could never be a vegetarian. I don't know how you do it. Is it even healthy?" Mankind possesses the technology to put a human on the moon, to harvest nuclear energy, and you still wonder if we have the appropriate technology to create and eat an adequate food supply without harming animals? It is an entirely attainable goal to acquire all nutritional sustenance from plant sources.

Carnivorous animals like lions and tigers have large canine teeth, short intestinal tracks, and strong stomach acids. Vegetarian animals like rabbits, monkeys, and cows have small canine teeth, long intestinal tracks, and weak stomach acids. Humans have small canine teeth, long intestinal tracks, and weak stomach acids. Anatomically, humans have more in common with vegetarian animals. The choice is clear on every level. Maybe at one point in time when mankind struggled for survival as a species eating meat was essential. We have evolved past that point and have begun to have a detrimental effect on the environment and our society because of our eating habits. Change is needed. Vegetarianism is not an unmaintainable diet; it is a globally transforming lifestyle solution that our survival as a society depends upon.

Make an Offering

"Cry to him with a yearning heart and you will see Him. Men weep a jug full of tears for their wives and children. And for money they shed enough tears to flood a river. But who weeps for God? Seek him with a loving heart." -Ramakrishna

To experience God, there must be a great yearning. You must orient all your desires toward knowing Him. You must want it so badly you cry for the experience late into the night in prayer or meditation. Want God until it hurts and He will ultimately answer the call, opening the gates to heaven within. Pure bliss awaits in this divine union.

All actions must be offered up to God. Eventually, you will be able to dedicate your very life itself as a sacrament to the Eternal. Take for instance eating. It is not adequate to just say a prayer before you eat. You must consciously take each bite of food not for yourself, but for the manifestation of God in you. How much you eat does not matter. The expense or quality of the food does not matter. It does matter that the food is pure (sattvic), and created with the proper intention and without harm. Each morsel of food you ingest is not for you, rather meant as an offering to the Creator. In this manner, you enjoy the food more and eat less.

The food offered to God through you transforms into the energy needed for divine service in the world. This way each action you take not only becomes sacred but is intentionally powered by your Higher Self. This can only be made possible when you chose to feed your Higher Self instead of your small self.

When I finish eating, I sing a devotional song out loud or silently to myself in honor of the communion just made. This allows me to heighten the sense of appreciation I have for God. In turn, I receive a clearer vision of how to best use His energy. Always remember, it is not me doing anything. When I do something, it is only my ego that is in operation. Instead chose to allow God to do His will through me. In this manner, all my actions are guided from an elevated perception. I take my ego out of the picture and humbly access the truth and wisdom of divine grace.

Living life consciously that we are actors in a celestial play allows the spiritual aspirant to hear and follow the cues of the heavenly director of the cinema of our reality. In your prayers, do no ask for your desires to be fulfilled. Instead as Christ prayed, ask for "Thy will to be done". Seek direction in your meditation by listening instead of making an order. Alternatively, make an offering of your life. This allows you to detach from the results as it is not you who is calling the shots. Guilt and judgment cease entirely when you recognize you are only following directions. By such means you become the master player in the earthly drama. God is reflected through everyone. When you serve others, you serve Him directly.

You do not have to be a saint or a monk to use the powerful techniques of prayer and meditation throughout the day. Whenever I feel discontent or unsatisfied with my current circumstance, I tune back into reality with my meditation practice. Maybe I am becoming frustrated with a student, starting to feel bored, or even believe I need to eat more than I did, I check in with my breath and start chanting my mantra. This can be done all throughout the day. Maybe this little meditation moment lasts only five minutes, even one minute. That is often all I need to tune back in to the ocean of peace that inevitably surrounds me in each moment.

When I stop living my life for me and opt to live it for God, the suffering or discontent ceases. Tranquility abounds and I forget my ego's expectation that every moment must be filled with fun and excitement. Most times the experience of peace give me a much more lasting sense of gratification than any temporary experience of excitement can boast. The more I check in with my meditation, the more I become grounded in peace. I attain the ability to share that sentiment with others by my mere presence alone. Ultimately, it is not my presence but that of something greater flowing through me. In a solar eclipse the moon passes before we can see the sun once again. In the same way, I must let my ego float away for my true self to illuminate the world.

Ramakrishna was an extraordinary holy man in 19th Century India. He taught, "Yearning for God is like the coming of dawn. Dawn comes before the sun itself rises. When yearning for God comes, the vision of God itself must follow." Think of how a materialistic man cares for money. How does a parent love a child? How does a spouse love a partner? Combine the intensities of these attachments and direct them toward God. Only then is divine communion possible.

Ramakrishna explained how the material world is akin to water and the mind to milk. Mixed together you cannot separate water from milk. When first you isolate the milk, and curdle it, it becomes butter. This butter floats on water. The same when we isolate the mind and apply the proper meditation techniques, the mind transforms and the material world loses its effect on the mind. At the point when one directs all energy toward the spiritual realm, self-realization becomes inevitable.

It is beneficial to dedicate some time just to yourself every now and again. Maybe a few minutes each day or a few days each month. Think of it as spiritual maintenance. When we maintain the connection to our Higher Self, achieving destiny becomes a reality.

Chapter 11: The Five Causes of Suffering

The kleshas are an idea that Patanjali discusses in the yoga sutras. The term represents the concept of the five afflictions of the mind. These are the causes of all suffering. These afflictions are created entirely within, the mind. Looking from the outside in, most of us would likely believe suffering comes from the external environment. This is not true. Although some are dealt seemingly better cards than others (this is a direct result of past impressions or karma), one's interpretation of his or her status in life is what determines whether suffering takes place. The mind is the interpreter between the soul (purusha) and the physical world (prakriti). You are exactly where you are supposed to be in life right now. That includes all the good and all the bad. Your current experience in life has hidden lessons guiding you to realize your purpose as you begin to clear the lens of the heart-mind (citta). These lessons alleviate past karmas and give you the opportunity to take your next evolutionary step forward.

The five afflictions of the mind are: avidya-ignorance, raga-attachment, dvesa-aversion, and abhinivesa-fear of death. Understanding these afflictions, analyzing their existence through your interpretation of life and developing a clear perception will alleviate suffering and create happiness in your life.

The kleshas are the cause of the thought process behind negative emotions. These kleshas are at the root of all unwarranted fear. Ignorance creates fear of the unknown. Ego creates fear of losing power. In attachment is the fear of not experiencing past pleasures again. In aversion exists a fear of past suffering. The most intense fear most people experience in life is anxiety regarding death.

It is very challenging to be honest enough to identify how these afflictions manifest in our own lives. It is incredibly liberating once we realize and correct these misperceptions. Just learning the notion of the kleshas provides a great sense of freedom. There are three methods to overcome mental afflictions. Tapas is some form of consistent daily spiritual practice that cultivates the fire of transformation. Svadhyaya is in-depth self-study that includes introspection and research of ancient wisdom teachings or sacred texts. Ishvara Pranidhana is surrendering to the will of the divine. Cultivating tapas, svadhyaya and ishvara pranidhana gives us the ability to broaden our perspective and clarifies the past impressions (samskaras) that smudge the lens of perception.

Our past impressions are what create non-working habits. Following this trail from the current state of our negative habits to their creations takes the individual on a journey back to his or her own source of truth. When these habits are undone, we bring clarity to our perception and our current reality is no longer clouded by past traumas. You begin to live and act with a consciousness rooted in the heart-mind connection. Your judgment ceases to be misguided by past suffering and you can focus on the more spiritual elements of life and live out your purpose.

Others are mirrors for us to see our true selves. When you act negatively toward another person there is a reason you reacted this way. A past experience conditioned you to react to the world in such a manner. Use this undesired reaction as an opportunity for a moment of self-study. Truly ask yourself why you acted in such a way. Was it because of something they did or were you reminded of a past experience? Be grateful to that person for being your mirror and permitting you an opportunity for growth.

At different times in life we experience different kleshas. Youth is filled with ignorance. As we come to know more and acquire more experience, the ego arises. In middle age clinging and aversion tend to be strong. Toward the end of life fear of death grows as it inevitability grows closer.

Avidya-Ignorance

Ignorance clouds consciousness like the fog covers the Northern California bay. The light of awareness is what burns off the mist. Vidya is the light of knowledge. In Sanskrit, when there is an "a" in front of a word it means the opposite of the root word. For example, vidya means knowledge, avidya means ignorance. Vidya is more than just scholarly knowledge. It is an inner awareness or intuitive knowing. This type of knowledge permeates from the light of our true self. Avidya or ignorance is the darkness of unconsciousness. Like a candle irradiates light throughout a dark room, knowledge illuminates ignorance.

Conditioning creates misperceptions that cause unconscious action. This keeps one from realizing truth and realizing purpose. Ignorance is truly the source of all suffering. It is the root or basis for all other kleshas.

The method to overcoming ignorance is through a consistent spiritual practice (abhyasa), conscious discernment (viveka), and non-attachment (vairagya). It requires great effort, discretion, and detachment from misguided beliefs. With this introspection, little by little you can clear up the cloud of ignorance and the light of knowledge will be uncovered. Maybe when you start this process of purification you will be 99 percent ignorant, day by day, through practice, discernment, and non-attachment your percentage will fall lower and lower until ignorance disappears and only knowledge remains.

Describing this process reminds me of when I decided to become vegetarian. At first, because of my belief system, I thought I could not survive without eating meat. How ignorant was I? My father suggested that if I was interested in vegetarianism, I should try it out for a day and see how I felt. After the first day, I felt amazing! My body seemed to operate more efficiently. I felt I had more energy from eating less food. After a week of consuming a vegetarian diet, I went back to eating chicken and fish, but not red meat. One year later, I stopped eating chicken. One year later, I gave up fish.

At first, my ignorance caused me to believe it was not physically possible for me to maintain a vegetarian diet. As I began to practice vegetarianism being more discerning of what I ate, and detaching myself from long held dietary beliefs, the ignorance began to go away little by little. It took a few years, but eventually I had the knowledge to transform my eating habits.

In your life, what belief systems have created misperceptions? Perhaps you can think of a past experience that led you to see the light or maybe you can identify a current misperception maintained by a false belief. How can a daily spiritual practice, discernment and non-attachment transform that ignorance to knowledge in your life?

Asmita-Ego

It's all about me, me, me. Asmita is a distorted sense of one's self. There are two forms in which asmita can manifest. A distorted sense of self can be expressed as an over-inflated ego or as a lack of self-esteem. The balance between self-esteem and modesty is realized through the death of the ego. Like a phoenix rising in its own ashes, through the death of the ego is the birth of humility.

It can be tricky to grasp a full understanding of the ego. The Bhagavad Gita relates taming the ego to lassoing the wind. Another wonderful analogy of the ego is an air bubble caught between water and a piece of plastic. When you press down on the bubble, it creates two bubbles. This is the ego. Some texts describe the ego as a thousand-headed snake. When you cut off one head, two grow back.

The thought process creates the ego and the ego then creates emotions. The ego is a modality of the mind, however neither is the Self. It is easy for perception to become distorted and identify with the mind or ego. Emotions are physical reaction to thoughts. Understanding instincts helps to increase apprehension of the idea of emotions. Instincts are a physical reaction to an external circumstance. Emotions are a physical reaction to the mental process. This explains physical reactions like shaking hands, sweating, pacing, and tunnel vision (among many others) when we experience anger or other emotions.

We must train ourselves to maintain the psychological stance of being the master of the mind instead of its slave. If we can watch our thought process take place and view our brain functioning from an objective point of view, we are obviously not the mind itself. This process plays out constantly during the practice of meditation. The practice eventually begins to beg the question "Who am I?" Realizing the answer to this inquiry is the basis for enlightenment. The Self is the Spirit of the universe itself. Attaining such knowledge is one thing. To live in realization of your source is to ascend to another dimension. Meditate on this question and you open yourself to the possibility of such a realization.

Watching a child grow is a good example to see the ego in play. When the child is very small there is no ego, only a connection or oneness with the world. We give the child a name and begin to give him or her possessions reinforcing the false belief that the individual is separate from the whole. Conditioning starts as soon as we are born and continues throughout an individual's lifetime. The truth is that the entire planet is one organism. The ego acts as a curtain separating the individual from union with the universe.

The ego encourages us to judge and blame, creating the belief we are better or worse than others instead of understanding that we are all in this journey together. The ego distorts the interpretation of reality. Some fears are validated. We developed fear for evolutionary reasons to keep us safe. Thousands of years ago, humans were afraid to go out in the dark because large, predatory, nocturnal animals were a threat to survival. At the time this was a valid fear, but this apprehension is no longer valid in modern society.

The ego often causes us to misinterpret fear, which increases suffering. This was very apparent in martial arts. As I became proficient in martial arts, my ego began to inflate. I began to train with a master jiu-jitsu practitioner who quickly taught me the error of my ways. The ego caused me to think I was better than I really was. Misinterpreting the warning signs when I trained with Master Baret usually culminated in a painful lesson in humility. When it comes to sports, there is always someone better or worse than you. In martial arts, I learned to take every opponent seriously and operate with the highest levels on mindfulness. Approaching each challenger with humility, I had greater ability to interpret each unique situation and stand victorious or at least avoid a little suffering. The matches I lost, were my best opportunities to learn, grow, and improve. Matches won served as occasions to practice humility.

On the opposite side of the coin, everyone at one time or another has experienced a lack of self-esteem. This is usually created by an inability to overcome obstacles. When you fall off the horse, it is imperative you get right back on without delay. Delay creates doubt, which destroys self-esteem. Paradoxically, those who desire to be better than others have an ingrained fear of not being as good as others. Those who are afraid of not being as good as others harbor the secret desire to be better than everyone else. Consciousness is all one. There is no good or bad; there just is. It is critical to recognize and respect everyone is at a different level in his or her own development.
Others serve as a mirror for us to see our own reflection. Instead of straining to compete with others, the spiritual being understands that everyone can succeed and work toward the success of the whole.

During one of my yoga teacher trainings, the group practiced helping students drop from a standing position into a backbend. I was working with a very experienced practitioner.

She has a big tattoo on her back of the Hindu God Ganesh (who represents the removal of obstacles). I was not confident of my ability to help and when assisting her in the movement, I dropped her on the ground very hard! I felt horrible about it. She jumped right up and said, "Don't worry Ganesh's got my back". Much to my dismay, she forced me to help her do it again. The second time I got it just right. I helped her back perfectly before doubt set in and I lost the self-esteem to help anyone else. It was a good thing she did that because the next day I had to help 30 people drop into backbends. I did not drop anyone and have not since.

To have a clear sense of self requires self-study (svadhyaya), daily practice (tapas), and surrender to the divine will (ishvara pranidhana). I find that when I remember I am in the passenger seat and God is the one driving, I tend to be much humbler. In the moment-to-moment consciousness of life is where we connect to the sense of humility. It requires constant awareness to be present, centered, and remember we are here to be of service to others. No one is better than anyone else regardless of one's social, racial, political, or economic status. We are all in this journey together.

Raga-Attachment

The next two kleshas have much in common. Clinging to attachment and aversion to suffering are two of the strongest kleshas and cause the most suffering. Both can be understood as forms of clinging. Raga is clinging to past pleasure. Dvesa is clinging to suffering.

It is normal to want to know a pleasing experience again. Suffering comes from not letting go of that pleasure. Clinging forces us out of the present moment. Clinging forces us to get stuck in past memories or future desires for pleasure. It is very difficult to chip away at Raga. The draw of our external senses is strong. Going inside, leaving attachment in the material world is the way to overcome raga. Patanjali's three step method of Kriya Yoga is the path to make the shift: daily practice, self-study, and surrender to God.

Experiencing a highly enjoyable event creates a memory that creates an attachment and culminates to a habit. As the attachment becomes stronger we repeat the action developing habits, or even stronger yet, addictions. In retrospect, the two instances in my own life where attachments seem to be most prominent are romantic relationships and drug addiction.

Relationships are a perfect example of raga in our society. The pleasure we experience with a partner often long outlasts the positivity and productivity of the relationship itself. Because we become so attached to an experience of past pleasure with a person we cling to the relationship, despite intolerable amounts of suffering.

In my early 20s, I dated a woman who was much older than me. In getting to know this older and more experienced woman, there were some physically pleasurable moments. Becoming attached to these momentary experiences clouded my judgment. Because I enjoyed the physical experience looking past the finer details in the relationship became habitual. I knew that she was older, already had children, and that our personalities and experiences in life did not match well. But because of attachment to physical pleasure, I looked past the important concerns about the relationship and suffered greatly. The suffering did not end until I ended the relationship for good.

When we develop emotional attachments, other people can look at our own lives objectively and with better discernment than we can. Attachment clouds our perception so we can no longer be honest with ourselves about what is best for us. It is important to consider the advice of those in your trusted inner circle.

Others asked me why I continued to stay in this relationship. I began to do self-study (svadhyaya), asking myself deeper questions about my future. Becoming honest with myself became a consistent practice (tapas). When I decided I was ready get to out, I went to my spiritual teacher who gave me advice on the best moves to make to cut ties with this woman. Surrendering to all potential outcomes and accepting whatever the results, I followed his advice (ishvara pranidhana). Humbling myself, I trusted that I would survive the experience.

Addiction is another extremely challenging hurdle in our society. The pleasure of food, drugs, sex or any other sensual experience can seem like an easy escape. Listening and researching the advice given to us by others is a great way to consider our subconscious (svadhyaya). By being consistently honest (tapas), we humble ourselves and surrender our power to God (ishvara pranidhana). In this instance surrendering is empowering. We merge our will with God's, finding a sense of purpose, and realizing a strength within never known to be accessible.

It is even possible to become so set in our own healthy habits that negative consequences arise. I have seen students become agitated if they miss their yoga asana or meditation practice. At times, I have been guilty of this. It really is quite paradoxical. We become so attached to a spiritual practice that is designed to decrease our attachment. Practicing yoga and meditation should increase physical and mental flexibility. But when we must do our practice just to be happy, it becomes a burden and we lose mental flexibility. The practice becomes an attachment and in this case, holds the practitioner back from spiritual progression.

My mother always told me, "Everything is good in moderation". This idea even includes spiritual practice. Selfstudy (svadhyaya) gives an opportunity to be accountable for afflictions of the mind. Consistent accountability (tapas) creates humility (ishvara pranidhana). In surrendering to something greater than ourselves, it is possible to know and live in gratitude. When daily introspection becomes habitual, we find union with God. That is the purpose of yoga. Seeking a balance between the physical and spiritual planes creates a fluid harmony in the life of the aspirant.

The Indian Saint Neem Karoli Baba gave a discourse on attachment to his students. They told him they never wanted to leave his presence and asked if this was attachment. He said, "No, this is love." The difference between love and attachment is that attachment is about control. Love is all about surrender. When you unburden yourself from attachment you rise in love.

Dvesa-Aversion

It is entirely normal to want to avoid suffering. Painful situations are designed to teach us to avoid experiences that could be detrimental to our well-being. There is a difference between pain and discomfort. All change is accompanied by discomfort. It is entirely necessary for growth. With discernment, it is possible to differentiate between pain and discomfort. The yoga asana practice is a great place to develop this skill. When practicing a challenging posture, you are pushing toward your physical limit. Because you are increasing your limitations, there will be an element of discomfort. If you push yourself past your limit, your body begins to contort its alignment and you experience the warning signs of pain.

An unhealthy form of aversion would be to stop practicing the posture because of the pain. The pain came from pushing past your limit. Using discernment, you realize the pain came from sacrificing your alignment to be goal oriented. The alternative to aversion in this situation comes through practicing with heightened consciousness in the posture, accepting your limitation, and maintaining the best alignment possible. Learn to remain open to the experience of discomfort. This mental and physical space creates a medium for growth. By respecting your limit, you define your boundaries. Decide where you want to go in life and determine how best to navigate the course.

Referring to the relationship example I wrote about in the section on raga, I overcame much aversion (dvesa). I was afraid to leave the relationship because of a fear of suffering, the fear of being alone. I had a fear this woman would be with someone else, perhaps even one of my friends. Unsubstantiated fears create the misperceptions that precede aversion. I had an aversion to end the relationship because I was afraid it would cause more suffering. Ending the relationship brought an end to much unnecessary suffering. Through consistent (tapas) selfstudy (svadhyaya), I came to a place of clearer perspective about the relationship. As I surrendered to the divine will (ishvara pranidhana), I found the strength and confidence to move forward with my life, creating and following through with the steps to end the relationship. The steps I mention were things like collecting my things, moving out, changing phone numbers, and staying positive among others.

Aversion rears its head in many places in life. When dealing with difficult coworkers, troubled friendships, and persistent family members the tendency toward avoidance is prevalent. Introspection allows us to identify when we are operating with dvesa. The methods of Kriya Yoga are invaluable to recognizing we are not living to our fullest potential getting the most out of all relationships, especially the most important one, the relationship with our self.

When battling addictions people often experience the strongest moments of dvesa. I smoked pot for 15 years and would do everything stoned (even practice yoga and meditation). I developed a fear that if I did not smoke I would suffer greatly. In part, this was true due to the incredible length of time I avoided dealing with the issue. My brain chemistry changed due to the prolonged consistency of my using. At first getting clear, the neuro-receptors in my brain were highly desensitized. Daily pot use trained my brain to be under sensitive to the chemical regulating happiness, serotonin. So being clean, I experienced less happiness doing the same things that always made me happy like yoga, hiking, and especially eating good food. I lost 15 pounds in the first month I stopped using pot.

Paying close attention to the workings of my mind (svadhyaya), I realized what was happening. Honestly evaluating the change I experienced daily (tapas), I found that my brain would slowly recalibrate and rebalance its own neurochemistry. The desire I had to experience the pleasure of pot again, and the aversion to dealing with my emotions, was strong. Surrendering my will to God (ishvara pranidhana), I discovered the strength and commitment to rise to the task and maintain sobriety. My brain function increased dramatically over the first few months. The 12-step program has a great deal in common with the method of Kriya Yoga. Relying on the support of friends and family, I received much assistance in overcoming deeply seeded habits and created everlasting change in my life. It is difficult to evaluate our own life because we are so emotionally connected. This is where trusting the guidance of a support group or inner circle is critical.

Whether you realize you are operating with aversion, attachment, unnecessary fear, ignorance, or ego, practice the methods of Kriya Yoga constantly. This allows you to stay grounded (tapas), evaluate the situations (svadhyaya), and humbly realize your purpose in this world (ishvara pranidhana).

Abhinivesa (Fear of Death)

I have often heard it said, "The only two things in life we are all guaranteed are death and taxes." In any case, with birth inevitably comes death. So where does the fear of death come from? The fear of death comes from attachment to physical body and attachment to the fruits of our life's labor. The attachment comes from the ignorance that the soul is eternal. It is embedded in our instincts. Without the fear of death, perhaps our species would not have evolved to where it is today.

Some fears are justified and some fear concerning death can be overcome with knowledge. A justified fear of death that we experience because of our evolutionary advancement might be the fear of confronting a large carnivorous creature, like a bear. Confronting a large hungry bear in the wild, you would experience a healthy fear of death that would motivate you in a way to act that hopefully keeps you safe.

What abhinivesa is hinting at is more of the fear of relinquishing the life we have created. This includes our family, social status, material and intellectual property, reputation, and other physical features. The ego is quick to cling to its existence. When we learn to let go of the ego and realize the liberation that accompanies the acknowledgement of our physical impermanence, death becomes just one more transitional step in the journey of our everlasting soul. The soul never dies.

The eternal soul manifests from the divine realm into the physical realm for only a blip of time in the immemorial existence of reality. We are only here in this body for a short parenthesis in the never-ending encyclopedia of the Universe. The soul enters the body to fulfill an important duty and to evolve to its next stage of development. There is no sense in being attached to the body or anything else in the impermanent realm, which is only meant to be temporary. Everyone is afraid of the pain of dying. In death, there is no pain. When the soul leaves the body, how could there be pain? The body and the mind are what feel pain. When the soul returns to its source there is no pain, there is only bliss. So why be afraid of death? Instead, at the moment of death, welcome the return to your source.

Our fear of death is based on our attachment to the material aspects of life. Due to our conditioning, we cannot differentiate our true self between thoughts, ego, the body, actions, and material possessions among many other forms in the realm of impermanence. If you think about it, you really do not anything. Something, whether it be money, a house, a car, a nice suit, or anything else you own, has come into your possession for only a small moment in time. You are just borrowing it. Instead, recognize and appreciate the blessing of enjoying these material comforts, because they are only temporary. To overcome this duality, surrender is the path. Control and ownership are only illusions. If you really think about the transitory nature of the process, wouldn't it be less painful to traverse your journey in peace instead of fear? All things we relate to in this world are entirely impermanent. Meditate on that which is eternal to connect with the divine light of awareness, the essence of the true self. Keep inquiring, "Who am I, who am I, who am I?"

Chapter 12: The Eight-Limbed Path to Enlightenment

The eight limbs, known as Ashtanga Yoga in Sanskrit, are pearls of wisdom strung together for the benefit of all mankind. These steps guide us through an attainable path to enlightenment. What is more amazing is that these steps, these ancient wisdom teachings continue to function from thousands of years ago through the present age.

Christ, Buddha, Mohammed, and the modern spiritual teachers impart their prophetic teachings with the intention of inspiring us to begin the journey inward. What is so special and unique about the teachings of Patanjali is that he was both poetic and scientific. His beautiful words follow the scientific method touching our hearts and leaving specific guidelines that give us the ability to follow in his footsteps on the road to enlightenment. The eight limbs continue to stand the test of time. As presented here, they will be in their entirety and as clear as possible for the modern seeker to interpret and utilize. Each limb sprouts in our lives like a limb or branch on a tree. They may not manifest in the exact order Patanjali gives us but each limb marks a waypoint or guideline for the attainment of knowledge of our true self.

Ashta-Eight Anga-Limbs

1. **Yama (Ethical Practices)**

    Ahimsa-nonviolence

    Satya-truthfulness

    Bramacharya-conservation of sexual/spiritual energy

    Aparigraha-non-covetousness

Yama is the first limb of Patanjali's eight-tiered system. The ethical practices guide the spiritual practitioner in how to peacefully coexist with others. As the foundation for the eight limbs, the yamas are a crucial beginning point of the journey. The yamas teach us to treat others how we want to be treated. A clear understanding and practice of the yamas develops compassion, gratitude and discernment. Misunderstanding of the yamas expresses itself as anger greed and bad judgment. The yamas guide us in how to operate with love and compassion toward others beings on our way to realizing we are truly all one sentient being.

-Ahimsa (non-harm)

Nonviolence is probably the most important ethical practice of them all. Thoughts create emotions, which create beliefs culminating in action. We should aspire toward nonviolence in every layer of our psyche. Analyze thoughts in challenging situations. Learn to recognize which thoughts are harmful or risky. With this heightened awareness, you can learn to disrupt the unconscious chain reaction from thought to emotions to beliefs and ultimately action.

An example I can discuss here is the common experience of a problematic coworker. Imagine you and this colleague are vying for the same promotions in a few months. The coworker constantly puts down your work to sabotage your efforts. You may think, "I'll show him. I can do the same. I will delete the files he has been working on for a big project. I have to get ahead of him." The emotions that arise are anger, jealousy, maybe even hatred. The belief created is, "I have to get ahead by any means necessary". The actions that result are less than honorable and if discovered by the company could result in your termination. Look at how harmful thoughts result in actions with the opposite results of the original intentions.

Look at how practicing ahimsa could improve this situation. When you find your coworker trying to disrupt you, catching the thought process in the act of becoming harmful, you consciously turn the tide. Transforming your mental activity, you tell yourself, "I understand why he is trying to cheat and will practice compassion. I need to stick to my morals. This is a test that can improve the quality of my work." Your emotions become empathetic. Your beliefs become reaffirmations of your system of values (in this case ahimsa or non-harm). Your actions demonstrate your determination and improve quality of your work. The result would likely be you receiving the promotion not only for the quality of work but also for your demonstration of leadership and having a strong moral compass. If you did not get the promotion for any reason, the workplace would remain relatively peaceful and productive.

When seekers begin practicing ahimsa, they could be 99% harmful in their lives. Little by little, with discernment, they make life less harmful and more compassionate. Vegetarianism is the traditional diet for a yoga practitioner. In my interpretation of this discipline, the practice of not eating meat is important to my practice of ahimsa. When a person eats meat, he or she obviously harms an animal either directly or indirectly. The person who had to kill the animal is harmed karmically. He harms himself through the creation of negative karma and by experiencing the negative health effect of eating meat has on the body (increased cancer risk, decreased digestion, elevated blood pressure and cholesterol just to name a few). He also creates a harmful effect on the environment.

On the yoga mat, I see many practitioners causing harm to their body by not honoring and respecting their physical limitations. The practice of yoga postures serves as an opportunity to practice ahimsa toward ourselves. One should not attempt to go beyond his or her limitation at the demand of the ego. Instead, ask your teacher for a variation of the posture or an alternative pose so that you can do to maintain your practice of ahimsa during your practice of asana.

It is easy to be nice to someone who is nice to you. This is not what ahimsa is about. It is saintly to be nice to someone who is mean to you. On the cross, Christ begged God's forgiveness for his wrongdoers. This is true ahimsa.

I once lived with a friend who got both of us evicted from our apartment because he paid his share of the rent late six months in a row. At first, I was very angry with him. I was literally homeless because of his actions. My anger began to turn to hatred, which paralyzed me. Buddha said, "Getting angry at someone is like grabbing a hot coal to throw at them and expecting them to get burned." When you feel a negative emotion toward someone, you are the one who suffers, not them. I was so angry that my emotional reaction prevented me from even beginning the search for a new place to live. A friend once reminded me of the true meaning of ahimsa and encouraged me to look for a compassionate place inside myself in dealing with this situation. When I was finally able to calm down and be honest, I admitted that the living arrangement was not ideal. The apartment was overpriced. My roommate and I were heading in different directions in our lives. Soon after I accepted reality, I quickly found a new home where I could live by myself in a more peaceful neighborhood. The townhouse I moved to was so much better for my spiritual practice and it greatly improved my quality of life. I cultivated a sense of gratitude toward my friend because my new living arrangement would not have been possible were it not for his actions. Cursing others, curses you. Blessing others brings a blessing to your life.

There is a wonderful story taught in the Jewish tradition about Jacob and the Israelites. Jacob's army put together a string of military victories, which greatly frightened his next opponent, Balak the king of Moab. Balak hired a magician named Balaam to curse Jacob and his people. Balaam meditated on God's desire and quickly realized God was on Jacob's side and did not want him to be cursed. But King Balak was very persistent and eventually Balaam agreed to do his bidding and curse the people of Israel.

Balaam rode a donkey toward a mountaintop overlooking the tents of Jacob to perform the curse. An Angel appeared before the ass and the animal refused to continue. Balaam rode in a different direction and the Angel appeared to the donkey twice more. Not able to see the angel, Balaam did not understand why his donkey was so uncooperative. He became enraged and began to beat the animal. God gave the donkey the power of speech, which perplexed Balaam. The donkey asked him why he beat her. Balaam was still furious at which point The Angel appeared to Balaam and told him to continue his journey but that he must do God's bidding, not Balak's.

Balaam arrived at his destination and was greeted by Balak. After an offering was made, Balaam prepared to make a curse but only a blessing fell from his mouth. Balak was furious and prepared another offering as he insisted Balaam curse the Israelites. Again, Balaam was only able to offer a blessing. God made it so only praise came out of his mouth. For the third time Balak prepared an offering and for a third-time Balaam was only able to bless the tents of Jacob.

When we bless others, we bless ourselves. Only one entity can bless and it is not the small self. It is the Highest Self or God. Free will and destiny are intertwined as everything in creation falls under the order of the cosmos. Nothing happens that the divine does not will into creation including blessings or curses. Balaam was a true spiritual seer who had surrendered his will to God. Therefore, his power came not from him, but rather from the Source. He could only do God's bidding.

-Satya (truthfulness)

The next ethical behavior is honesty or truthfulness. More than stating correct facts, this yama implies we act in accordance with the truth. Satya is especially powerful when practiced in accordance with ahimsa. With a non-harmful state of mind, it becomes much easier to live the virtues of the yamas. You would not be likely to steal if you were honest about being non-harmful in all your actions toward others. When our thoughts, speech, and actions manifest in alignment, we are expressing truth in all aspects of the self.

It is important to be honest with others as well as with ourselves. If others come to you for advice on a difficult matter, it is best to give them straight-forward advice and not sugarcoat the truth. Even if their feelings may suffer a little in the short run, you are likely saving them greater suffering in the long term. Living in ignorance creates greater long-term suffering than living in awareness.

Being honest with ourselves can be even more challenging. Regarding admitting and transforming our flaws, we must be rigorously honest with ourselves to identify our shortcomings. A person with a drinking problem must first admit they have a problem before they have any hope of overcoming the problem.

Practicing honesty also means avoiding gossip and not criticizing others behind their back. Before jumping to any conclusion and creating misperception, properly evaluate the situation using discernment to cultivate the clearest possible understanding of the truth.

-Asetya (non-stealing)

This yama is exactly as it sounds. One should refrain from taking what is not rightfully theirs. You should only accept what is rightfully yours and earned by honest means. Not taking can be discussed in many different aspects. Taking could be stealing some physical item like someone else's car. It could occur in a more benign form such as interrupting a conversation or stealing someone else's intellectual property. One way or another, we should not take what does not rightfully belong to us.

In our society, we are so caught up with ownership and being attached to the fruits of our labor. It would serve us well to remember that nothing in the physical world is permanent. You can only own your house for lifetime, if that. It is more important to have gratitude for those who were essential in helping you to achieve success. We should offer the fruits of our labor to God. Everything in this world is fleeting and impermanent. The results of our actions are determined by something much greater than ourselves. When Christ was asked whether one should pay taxes he responded, "Give to Caesar what belongs to Caesar, and give to God what belongs to God." We would not want to be taking from the Divine, now would we? Only that which is cheap and superficial can temporarily belong to any man. The purest aspects of existence like love, truth, and purity will always belong to God.

Bramacharya (conservation of energy)

I have alluded before to physical beings existing as vibration. This is the same as us being energy. This energy is sacred and should not be wasted. Bramacharya refers to conserving spiritual and sexual energy. Learn to channel energy upward by turning away from external sensory stimulation. We need our senses to function in the world but becoming attached and identifying with these senses prevents us from union with the Supreme. If we are focused on God, we are less likely to be overcome with sensual or material desire. When you experience physical desire direct it toward God. Learn to lust for communion with Him.

Sensual desire is powerful. Tantric practices and meditations channel sexual energy (from the second chakra) toward the spiritual center (the seventh chakra). When sexual desire is too strong, we act in inappropriate ways that encourage misguided decisions and can result in ruining relationships. Imagine you have strong feelings for someone and are ready to take the relationship to the next level, but the other person was not yet ready for that depth of commitment. These feelings could lead you to become emotionally or even physically forceful. It would be much better to practice controlling this energy (Bramacharya) and respecting the others person's needs. This allows the potential of the relationship to grow in a much healthier environment.

Fasting from eating, taking a media break, refraining from intercourse for a specific length of time, and spending a dedicated amount of time in silence are all excellent practices to conserve and heighten awareness of our own spiritual energy. Conservation allows you to heighten your energy so you can use it when it is most appropriate. In Southern California, collectively using less electricity in the winter means more electricity will be available in the hot summer months and there will not be power blackouts. The same is true with spiritual energy. When a person preforms austerities conserving energy when they have the time and capacity, more of this energy will be available when required by future endeavors.

Aparigraha (non-grasping)

Aparigraha can be described as non-grasping of our thoughts, non-hoarding of possessions, and non-coveting others' possession. Aparigraha has much do with the entitlement created by the ego. The distorted sense of self (aka the ego) creates the idea that I am separate from everyone and everything else and is the basis for aparigraha.

The more we have, the more we feel we need. I am not describing a real need here, rather an unsubstantiated desire. If a person makes $1 million, he or she will spend much more money than if that person only had $1,000. Soon, the person will feel the need for $2 million and then $4 million, perpetuating the cycle of unsubstantiated needs. To overcome this affliction one must learn to detach from the fruits of his or her labor, working simply for the service of others, and finding happiness in that. Native Americans had a difficult time understanding the first Europeans who came to North America. The indigenous people saw the desire in the Europeans for more land than they could ever use and described the syndrome as a mental disorder or disease. It seems many in Western society today are still afflicted with this disease.

When we are grasping for material things, we create a lack of abundance in our lives. When we covet the physical body, it brings us out of balance and has negative effects on our health. Being possessive over our thoughts and ideas gets us stuck and prevents us from helping others.

The ego creates the idea of control and possession. Everything is constantly changing. When we realize, nothing is ever permanently ours, it becomes easier to release control. If I own a piece of property, I may come to create a sense of entitlement, ownership, coveting what I feel belongs to me. But the earth belongs to everyone. I am only here temporarily. Someone else will utilize this land after me.

We should not attempt to control others thoughts or actions. Everyone deserves the opportunity to create his or her own opinion on a social or political issue. It is alright to share your opinion with them, but allow them to form their own conclusion. Allow others to make their own decisions and follow through with their actions. Again, it is perfectly fine to give someone guidance or describe your personal experience, but they are on their own spiritual journey and living the effect of their own karma. They deserve the right to make their own decisions.

2. Niyama (Ethical Observances)

Sauca-cleanliness

Santosha-contentment

Tapas-heat created by practice

Svadhyaya-self study

Ishvara Pranidhana- Surrender to God

Niyama means ethical observance. As the result of the yamas is ultimately directed toward others, the effect of the niyamas is a set of internal disciplines focusing on ourselves. The niyamas are both internal and external observances. The first two observances are cleanliness and contentment, which includes gratitude. The final three niyamas are the trio that makes up the system of Kriya Yoga-daily spiritual practice, selfstudy, and surrender to the divine will.

To be of service to anyone else, we must first take care of ourselves. Teaching yoga can be challenging. I have seen some teachers take on teaching more than 25 classes a week. With all that teaching, where is the time for their personal yoga practice? Without practicing your own spiritual discipline, how can you help someone else? The entire purpose of the eight limbs is to achieve the goal of spiritual practice. Enlightenment is the goal. The niyamas are the second step in the path to get us there.

Sauca (cleanliness)

The first niyama is sauca or cleanliness. This refers to both inner and outer, physical and mental cleanliness. Outer cleanliness means keeping our physical environment clean. An example would be not allowing our home to be filled with clutter or even vacuuming the carpet on a regular basis. We must maintain our hygiene like showering and brushing our teeth daily. The food we eat should be clean and sattvic because that directly effects our inner body. A vegetarian diet is recommended for the utmost adherence to sauca. If our body is our temple, we must be strict and regimented in maintaining its cleanliness. The body is a vehicle by nature that is not clean.

Our cars must be washed and kept up on a regular basis as the wear and tear of regular use makes them unclean. Our bodies must be cleaned regularly as they are always in use and will never really be completely clean, at least physically.

By inner cleanliness, I am referring to the mind and maintaining clean, healthy, positive thoughts. It is easy to fall into the habit of thinking unclean thoughts, to eating in an unhealthy way, or to be tired of cleaning all the time. When we monitor the vibrations, we put in our mind through the media, it makes it easier to control our desires. Watching television constantly bombards us with fast food commercials putting thoughts of unclean eating in our mind. This is just one example. Watching movies with violence or highly sexual content is another example. In general, the less television you watch, the less likely you are to be influenced by external sources to maintain unclean thoughts. Discernment is crucial in maintaining mental cleanliness.

When we learn to accept uncleanliness is a part of life, it becomes easier to accept that cleaning is a part of life too. Creating a habitual, timely routine like cleaning the house or car once a week is a good way to manifest cleanliness in life on a regular basis. A clean external environment helps us to have a cleaner body and thought process. A clean external world makes it easy for us to create a cleaner internal world. Just like we must clean our teeth every day, we must also maintain a daily spiritual practice like meditation or yoga to help cleanse our mind. Making a routine out of cleanliness gives you the ability to achieve and maintain both inner and outer purity.

Santosha (contentment)

The quality of life is determined to a great degree by our outlook. Life is either a glass half full or a glass half empty. The lens through which we perceive the world greatly influences what is seen. When viewed through the spectrum of gratitude, life becomes heavenly and facilitates the progress of the journey on the path of the eight limbs.

Contentment arises from humility and gratitude. Humility prohibits the ego from distorting the expression of the divine will in our lives. Gratitude happens when we stand in awe and appreciation of the magnificence of experiencing that will. Contentment is the sense of peace you will know in living with God. Nothing is either perfect or permanent, but you deserve to allow yourself the satisfaction of accepting the present moment.

Contentment does not sprout from having your ideal job, income, or spouse. It does not come from a vacation, a new car, or an expensive outfit. Contentment is not created by any material means. It is a mindset or state of being created by cultivating and understanding of unity with the divine. This understanding allows us to comprehend the relevance of each moment and each experience in the greater scheme of things. When we are content, we are always moving forward because we are playing an active part in the creation of the divine expression.

Spending time in nature is a great way to cultivate the quality of contentment and gratitude. Nature is life expressed unadulterated truly as it was intended to be.

When I feel discontent, I practice a very simple meditation to improve the clarity of my perspective. I write down 10 or even five things that I am grateful for. This may sound too simple to be effective, but try it the next time you are feeling melancholy. If I drive a car that was a later model vehicle and always have problems I may start to develop a sense of selfpity. This gratitude-in-action meditation would be applicable. I could write: 1) I am grateful to have a vehicle. 2) My car gets me everywhere I need to go. 3) I am grateful I have a job to go to. 4) I appreciate all the places I have gone in my car. 5) Driving this car saves gas and I appreciate it has a lower impact on the environment.

My perspective instantly shifts from one of self-pity to one of gratitude and contentment when I apply the magic of this meditation. With practice, it becomes easier to stay content all the time. Being content allows us to stay open to receiving God's blessings on a regular basis. Being grateful lets the universe know we appreciate what we receive and are ready to receive more.

The next three niyamas are grouped together under the umbrella of Kriya Yoga. These niyamas used together are a cure for the kleshas or afflictions of the mind (which were discussed earlier). They are tapas, svadhyaya, and ishvara pranidhana.

Tapas (practice)

An exact translation for the word tapas does not exist in English. The term refers to the purification process. heat created by preforming a spiritual practice. This term can be used to describe the yoga asana (posture) practice. In an intense physical yoga practice, our body creates internal heat that burns off toxins in our system through sweat, urine, or excretion.

The term could also be used to describe the mental process that one undergoes in meditation. Watching our thoughts, searching for stillness, requires intense devotion. Cultivating devotion is akin to kindling a fire. A spark ignites passion, the breakthroughs we experience add small twigs to build the fire. The heat (tapas) created burns off mental impurities (false perceptions) leaving us with a clearer view of ourselves and the world around. Tapas requires time and effort to accumulate. Overcoming a habit is not easy. Discomfort is part of the process. You must realize the difference between pain and discomfort. Pain is a form of suffering that hurts you and prolongs your journey. Discomfort is a form of suffering that encourages growth. Discomfort is a good thing. Pain is not. Nothing ever changes without the catalyst of discomfort.

Accepting discomfort facilitates the ability to be present during the experience heightening consciousness.

Tapas can be created by many different practices. For an abhyasi (yoga practitioner) it may be preforming asana or pranayama. For an alcoholic seeking sobriety, it could be attending an Alcoholics Anonymous meeting. For someone trying to lose weight, it might be running or going to the gym. For someone with a self-esteem issue it could be listening to a motivational speaker. Identify ways in your life to light your fire and keep it lit. This is the process that will manifest change. To make a positive change, set your intention and create a time structured plan of action to achieve your goal. With consistent effort and the willingness to experience a little discomfort, you will create the heat necessary to generate change in your life.

Svadhyaya (self-study)

Svadhyaya is any form of introspection or self-study. The practice (tapas) gives us a forum to look at our mind. Building the fire illuminates our internal space so we can take an honest look at our true selves. There are many forms of selfstudy. You can read books or listen to discourses from a Guru. Watching the mental process during a meditation or yoga practice gives us the insight to understand our ingrained modus operandi. Watch how you respond in situations. Do you think about what you say before you respond or do you just blurt out the first thing that comes to mind? Do you react or respond when experiencing fluctuations of your emotions?

In svadhyaya we get a chance to look at our conditioning (samskaras). We react in a certain way for a reason. Past experiences can condition us to respond in an unconscious, mechanical way to a common situation. Self-study gives us the opportunity to look at the root to those tendencies and loosen their grip on our psyche.

An example in my life is when I was very young I got sick and vomited after eating pickles. My entire life, I experienced an intense feeling of disgust every time I saw pickles. In my late teens, I decided to retry the food and surprisingly enjoyed it. The experience I had when I was young discolored my perception and kept me from enjoying something I potentially could have appreciated all these years. This is a relatively benign example, but it would not be difficult to think of a much more harmful example. With svadhyaya, we can identify the source of our misperceptions and correct them. Realizing that we are not our thoughts and actions takes us a step closer to our true self. Our thoughts always change. The true self is eternal.

Ishvara Pranidhana (surrender to the divine will)

This is such a beautiful concept. Just say the words and you feel their beauty- ishvara pranidhana. The ego wants us to follow its will, make all decisions and, be the driver of the chariot of our mind. This course of action is one of a separated state of mind. Truly, there is only one predestined path, duty. This is our dharma and it is understood most clearly when we surrender our will and all fruits of our labor to God.

It is a great burden to take on all the responsibility for all the results we accumulate in life. Surrender is a great relief and can help us by creating some breathing room. When we try to take on all responsibility for all the results we accumulate in life, we experience a great deal of shame because not everything goes our way and our perspective becomes very narrow. From God's point of view the purpose of all things can be seen. Often, the reasons we must overcome extremely challenging situations in life is to learn lessons that we need to evolve spiritually. When we limit our thought process to the realm of only what our mind can deduce, we will never experience the metaphysical realm. We will never be able to take a leap of faith. The metaphysical realm is beyond the understanding of the body and mind. This does not mean that a world beyond the physical does not exist; merely the metaphysical is a realm subtler than most have yet been able to access. To find that place of surrender to the divine is incredibly empowering. You do your duty, what in the heart you know is right, and the responsibility for all results, good and bad, are left up to God. In challenging situations, there is no need to stress because there is a reason, an inherent purpose in all things. When you surrender, you give up the attempt to control that which enslaves you, and in turn gain a deeper understanding of where freedom exists. Surrender is the path to understanding, understanding illuminates purpose and purpose is the reason for existence.

      The opposite of surrender is fighting. I am reminded of my martial arts training. A fight is tit-for-tat. Your opponent hits you; you hit your opponent. In jiu-jitsu (which translated to the gentle hand), I learned that to win a fight, you must surrender. At first, this was a strange concept for me. To be successful in a fight you must surrender. When your opponent hits you, you react by hitting back. If you surrender to the fear of the results of your opponent's attack, you can respond (instead of react) with the correct technique to deflect the attack and neutralize your opponent. You win the fight of life when you learn to surrender to the fear. When you learn to surrender, you learn to truly live, to respond, to operate with an illuminated perspective. In the ability to surrender exists the potential for liberation.

      Surrender leads directly to enlightenment. You will learn to overcome the ego, a false belief of separation. In enlightenment, you will see the connectedness in all things. Overcome the ego by surrendering your control, what you perceive as power. It is an illusion. To surrender is to empower yourself and connect with the universe, to be enlightened.

The word "Ishvara" represents the source of all universal knowledge. "Pranidhana" represents the humility we experience when we surrender to something greater than ourselves. The existence of humility is the absence of the ego. Understanding this concept is the attainment of the knowledge that overcomes ignorance. All knowledge that comes through us belongs to the universe and came by way of the universe. All the honor of that knowledge belongs to those teachers from whom you channeled that knowledge in the first place. Devoting your actions to God allows you to be more discerning and reap the fruits that God desires for you.

What if you do not believe in God?

I will answer this question with another question. Is the earth greater than you? Is the universe greater than you? Your answer to this question is most likely yes. If your answer is no, the mental affliction of the ego is creating great ignorance in you. How great is the entire planet? And that does not even compare to the universe. At the grossest level, gravity is the order of the universe guiding and directing planetary movements, which directly influences life on earth. There are many more levels of order guiding us in more subtle levels. Recognize that there is a power greater than the individual self constantly at play and surrender to that power. Your meditation will reveal the secrets of the universe to you.

The act of surrender, regardless of the title of what you are surrendering to, is an act of humility. Through humility comes the power of faith. Humility helps you to overcome the ego and shine the light of awareness in you, burning off the cloud of ignorance like the sun burns off the early morning fog. There is great peace to be found in surrender.

3. Asana (Posture)

The third limb of Ashtanga Yoga is asana or yoga postures. When most people in the West think of yoga they identify with the postures taught in a yoga class. Although the postures are an important aspect of yoga, in truth asana is only one aspect of a much larger process. The purpose of practicing asana is purification, to make the body healthy. Specifically, the body needs to be limber enough to sit in the lotus posture or cross-legged comfortably long enough to create a meditation. That is the original purpose of asana. You need a healthy body to have a healthy mind to have a healthy spirit. All aspects of ourselves are tied together and it all begins with the body.

When I talk about a healthy body, I do not mean a beach body. It is sad to see in the West many who practice physical yoga only use it to increase their attachment to the physical body. The intention behind the practice should not be to have a physically attractive body, which is an insignificant side effect. As the purification process takes place through the physical yoga practice, the body becomes lighter, energetic pathways open, the mind becomes more calm. The physical body is better prepared as a vehicle to facilitate a deeper meditative practice toward the goal of illumination.

In the physical body runs a system of energy channels called nadi's. Due to psycho-somatic trauma (the source could be physical or emotional) blockages are created in this system known as granthi's. Preforming yoga postures allows us to tune into our physical and emotional trauma and unlock the granthi's creating a clear pathway for our prana to flow. For me, practicing yoga asana is a physical practice that allows me to align my physical, mental, and spiritual bodies.

The exact translation for asana is "seat". In the eight limbs, asana comes before pranayama (a form of deep breathing practice), so the practitioner can cultivate the ability to process the energy developed in pranayama. A good analogy to explain this phenomenon would be the wiring in a house. Imagine a house is wired to utilize 110 volts (residential power), and then you switch over the electrical current to 220 volts (commercial power) before rewiring the house. What happens is all the fuses blow out and the home cannot utilize the electricity. Practicing asana is analogous to the process of rewiring the house. Asana prepares the body to handle greater magnitudes of energy or prana. Pranayama runs a stronger current of energy through our body. This energy is utilized during later limbs in Patanjali's system to create and maintain a meditative state.

In asana, we start turning our focus inward with the breath while staying grounded in the physical body. In pranayama, we selectively work with the breath. In later limbs, the physical body is entirely unnecessary as it has already been purified and the process becomes completely internal.

Patanjali does not place a great emphasis on asana. In fact, he only mentions asana in two of his sutras. He says "yoga stirra asanam sukasanam". This infers a yoga posture should be performed with both steadiness and ease. A posture should be practiced with appropriate effort and appropriate surrender. We should practice this philosophy in our lives as well. There is no such thing as a perfect posture. The practitioner should be searching for the correct state of the posture. This refers to practicing postures in alignment with the appropriate physical and emotional surrender. In most postures, there is an actively engage contracted muscle group and a muscle group that is elongating or stretching. When we practice seeking alignment instead of gratification of the ego, we are practicing as Patanjali intended.

Yoga asana is designed to purify the physical body to prepare us for the next stage. Be compassionate and patient with yourself. Practice under the guidance of an experienced teacher and you will reap the many benefits from an asana practice.

4. Pranayama (Deep Breathing Practice)

Pranayama is the practice of regulating the breath. Prana is our life force. In other traditions, prana is also known as spirit, chi, or qi gong. The breath is the most essential element to life. Without food, we can live a month. Without water, we can live a week. Without air, we can live only minutes. It is said, we are born with a specific number of breaths fated to each lifetime. Through regulation of the breath, it is possible to lengthen our lives. Whether this notion is fact or fiction, taking longer deeper breaths allows one to be calmer. The more relaxed a person is, the longer and likely more peaceful their life will be.

Bringing our awareness to our prana with practices such as asana and pranayama turns our awareness from the physical body (Anamaya kosha) to the next most subtle layer of the self, the breath body (the pranamaya kosha). Consciously tuning into the breath begins our journey inward toward the self. Prana is the active source energy that moves within the nadi system and with proper practice and intention one can unlock granthisknots in the physical body and blockages in the metaphysical body that obstruct the flow of our spiritual energy. Pranayama is traditionally taught after practicing asana so that lung capacity is increased, which makes holding your breath easier. Once learned, it is preferred to practice pranayama before asana to improve the quality of breath throughout the asana practice.

Specific techniques and practices for complete sequences of pranayama routines should be learned in person from a qualified instructor. The first technique I learned (which had a profound effect on my life) was focusing on the rise and fall of the breath within my body. First focus your awareness on your toes and imagine your breath enters your body as a clear white light as you inhale. Follow this light all the way to the top of your head. As you exhale follow the light back down from your head to your toes. Repeat the process as many revolutions as you like (it could be for five breaths or 20 minutes). Notice how your awareness shifts from your physical body to the energetic body.

To take this experience deeper, it would be best to learn the pranayama practice from an experienced instructor. Different bandhas (internal locks) are used during pranayama to direct the flow of prana. Mula Bandha (root lock) is engaged by recreating the action used when holding it when you need to urinate. This is like the Kegel technique. Udiyanda Bandha (flying upward lock) is engaged by pulling the navel toward the spine. Jalandala bandha (throat lock) is made by dropping the chin toward the chest. These locks are effectively used during asana and pranayama. When all three locks are used simultaneously, they create a mahamudra, or great seal. In asana, the bandhas act as a tool to help us maintain correct posture and protect our physical anatomy. In pranayama, the bandhas assist to control retaining the breath. It is easier to focus on engaging the bandhas than to focus on the act of holding the breath. These locks direct the energetic current of our breath during the practice.

Practicing pranayama is extremely calming. There are three actions during pranayama: inhaling, exhaling, and retaining the breath. Inhales are stimulating. Exhales are relaxing, and retentions are centering (although some may say retentions are excruciating). The practice improves the relation between the practitioner and his or her prana. Pranayama turns our awareness inside toward our energetic self and greatly prepares us for the next limb, pratyahara (sense withdrawal). Pranayama creates an opportunity to shut out the external world and journey inward as the practitioner directly experiences the realm of pranic energy in turn overcoming mental fluctuations. When you find your mind running during the practice, bring your awareness back to the melody of your breathing. You will realize your breath is the music of life.

5. Pratyahara (Sense Withdrawal)

The fifth limb is a crucial transitory point. It demarcates the point in the process where our focus shifts from an external practice to a more internal method. The first four limbs are referred to as the lower or external limbs. Limbs five though eight are referred to as the upper or internal limbs. It is said a seeker keeps living life after life, relearning the lessons of the lower limbs until he or she finds a Guru or teacher who guides them to break the barrier deepening their journey in the eight limbs on the path to enlightenment. The further we go on this journey, the less words possess the ability to describe the experience. The lower limbs are external practices easily discussed in the physical world. The internal practices are experiences that have a depth that defies language. Your own experience is the only accurate means of truly understanding such profound realms of awareness.

In pratyahara, the practitioner blocks out the external world of the senses and truly begins the spiritual journey of the inner world. In the lower limbs, you cultivate the strength to focus. With consistency and devotion to the practice, little by little, you gain the ability to go deeper within yourself for longer periods of time and remain undisturbed by the external world. Imagine you are sitting practicing meditation and a fly in the room keeps disturbing you. You are starting to develop the ability to focus and go inside even when the fly lands right on your nose, and poof your attention diverts back outside. This is example accurately represents the struggle of our modern world. It may be a fly, the kids, the brakes of a car driving by, the television in another room. A spiritual discipline is traditionally practiced early in the morning before the majority of the world starts moving. This is what works best for me.

There are things we can do to limit these distractions. Find a time and place for your spiritual practice that best accommodates the inner space you are trying to create. Meditation, pranayama, and asana are traditionally practiced early in the morning before the world wakes up. This is what works best for me. Practicing before the outer world begins its customary commotion allows the practitioner to realize their intention. Maybe you practice while the kids are at school. If you work very early in the morning, maybe you practice at night. Set a schedule that works best for your life.

Pratyahara is not something that you can consciously preform. Think of it more as a result of a consistent practice. By sitting and focusing on your breath in pranayama or asana, your awareness gradually shifts from the outside in. You cannot say you are going to practice pratyahara. "Do your practice and all is coming" as Patthabi Jois used to say often. Pratyahara is the culmination of a consistent practice preformed accurately.

When pratyahara happens, the outer world loses its effect on you. The brakes squeaking on the cars driving by, or the sound of the TV in the next room do not disturb you because your focus is inside. We learn to turn off our external senses and activate the inner sensory world. The things that make you happy begin to change. Watching an action movie may not seem as enjoyable as reading a spiritual book. You become more comfortable spending time by yourself in silence. Naturally our senses focus outward. With the evolutionary process of the eight limbs, we learn to turn them inward. It is easy to get lost in the hurry of the modern world. The powerful practice of Ashtanga Yoga give us the superhuman ability to turn our focus inward in the modern culture of momentary consciousness, awareness becomes powerful and flows like the steady current of a might river.

6. Dharana (Concentration)

The sixth limb is concentration. Once we begin to withdraw focus from our external senses, we start to cultivate a space for meditation (the seventh limb). To prepare the ground of our mind for a bountiful harvest, concentration is needed. When most of us hear the word concentration, we associate the word with intense focus. This is an adequate definition. Another way to look at dharana is a process concentrating of our energy (prana). Earlier, I used the analogy of rewiring a house when using asana to prepare for pranayama. The same analogy could be used for dharana and dhyana (meditation). The intense concentration of our prana prepares our physical and metaphysical bodies to handle the effects of an actual meditation.

The sixth limb takes immense patience, months and more likely years to master. You will earn a degree in patience and will power as you establish yourself in dharana. As Patanjali described asana, it will require appropriate effort and appropriate surrender so too will dharana. Always remember to be compassionate to yourself.

In dharana, we learn to focus our attention on a single point. This point could be internal or external. What matters is that you fix your attention and do not deviate from your course. When you find your mind wandering, bring it back to the original point of focus. Your focus point could be a picture of a saint, a Hindu deity, a candle, Buddha, or any other element. Choose your point of focus with great discernment, as we become that which we focus our attention toward.

A disciple once went to his Ramakrishna and told him, "Every time I try to meditate, I keep thinking of my beloved pet bull." The Ramakrishna said to his student, "Well then focus on your pet bull during meditation." The Guru did not see his disciple for many months so he went to the man's home to check on his well-being. Ramakrishna stood in the doorway and upon seeing the student asked him to come outside. The disciple said, "I would, but my horns cannot fit through the door."

We become that which we focus on. Direct your focus on something that heightens your spiritual energy. Your true nature is God. The Bible says that God created us in his own image and truly we are a divine manifestation of the creator. If you focus on material things like money, a nice house, or a fancy vacation, you will attain those things. In fact, that is what our society teaches us to do. But if you choose to focus on these aspects, you will remain in bondage to the material world. To manifest freedom in your life, focus on your true self, your highest self, God. God is love. So, love is a great focus point for your meditation. Your chakras manifest metaphysical energy in the physical world. If you like, you can also focus on the chakras during meditation. Choose a pure (sattvic) point of focus and put steady effort into your meditation practice. To harvest fruit, you must water the tree daily. To create a real meditation, you must practice daily. With the correct intention and appropriate effort and surrender, you will create God's desired results in your life. Get comfortable and be patient. You will discover the journey can be just as enjoyable as the destination.

Despite the 6th and 7th limbs of Ashtanga Yoga taking the practitioner in the same direction, concentration and meditation are very different practices.

In concentration, one is focusing awareness to gain knowledge. You concentrate when you are studying for a test, to learn all the facts to earn a passing grade. Concentration requires concerted effort, focus and dedication. The point of our focus may not be entirely enjoyable or entertaining, but we practice to end suffering. A meditation does not stimulate the external senses so that we may redirect our awareness to a subtler inner dimension.

In a meditation, we are unlearning what we learned while concentrating. How can this be? A meditation is listening. It is learning how to listen actively. Imagine you are in a philosophy class and the instructor presents a moral question you have strong feelings about. Let's say the discussion is about the existence of God. Before the instructor says a word, you already have your mind made up. This is a result of societal conditioning. Perhaps, your family, culture or upbringing has led you to believe one way or another regarding the issue. This being the case, you will not believe or be open to learning anything the instructor says. You may hear the words he said, but your mind will interpret those words with whatever bias

you have been conditioned by. Philosophy is understanding all sides of a problem. In meditation, you unlearn your past conditioning so you may achieve a new level of understanding.

This is what is meant by when you concentrate, you learn. When you meditate, you unlearn. "Un" is the perfect prefix to use when describing a meditation. Meditation "un" conditions the mind. People live their entire lives in a state of conditioning or hypnotization without being aware of it. Meditation allows us to undo our inherent, automated programming and attain higher levels of understanding and awareness. Meditation gives us the ability to consciously live life and exist in the present moment, ascending beyond concerns of past or future experience. The experience is exactly where you are, in the here and now.

Concentration is a necessary predecessor to meditation because without it, you won't have the heightened ability of focus required to break through the veil of illusion. To create a real meditation requires a great deal of time and effort.

7. Dhyana (Meditation)

Taking another step closer toward samadhi (enlightenment), we create the experience of meditation. Most people who practice meditation think they are experiencing a meditation. The practice and experience of meditation are two very different realities. When you practice meditation, the mind continues to wander and we are still attached to our thought patterns. We do not yet understand the distinction between our thoughts and ourselves.

A meditation happens when, through immense effort and patience, we have created a state of continued focus. You start by stilling the body. When you begin to still the body, your eyes want to move. The eyes are the most external part of the brain. Still your eyes by focusing them on one fixed point or by closing them all together. If closed, focus your eyes at the point in between your eyebrows. Eventually, you will get to a place where you can still the mind. The Bhagavad Gita says that it is more difficult to still the mind that it is to lasso the wind. Continue expanding the focus you created in the sixth limb. Be compassionate with yourself and a meditation will come. In Dharana, we focus on one point. In dhyana, we merge into oneness with the point of focus, God. If you focus on the bullseye long enough, you will eventually hit the target.

In dharana, our awareness trickles like a stream. In dhyana, awareness flows like a roaring river. In samadhi, our consciousness becomes like a drop of water falling into the ocean of love.

The deeper you traverse on this journey, the more comfortable you become spending time by yourself. Solitude and silence become welcome, peaceful tools for introspection and improving the quality of meditation. Do not be alarmed by the sensation of withdrawing from the social limelight. Your focus begins to shift toward something much more meaningful and everlasting than what the general populace is doing. Not everyone is ready to take the spiritual path. Your focus becomes entranced with the notion of divine communion. Who cares about social media when you can learn to have a direct line of communication with the creator? How enticing is a night of drinking or partying when you know you possess the ability to see the world as Christ saw it? Drugs and alcohol give you a momentary high. This is a cheap, impermanent experience that only boasts negative consequences. Meditation will introduce you to your highest self, and the experience will not be temporary. You learn everything about yourself, who you really are. You can disassociate with the afflictions of your mind. Instances of ignorance, ego, attachment, aversion, and fear in your life flash before your eyes as you take the opportunity to forgive yourself for any past transgressions. You let it all go as you gravitate toward peace. Self-compassion manifests in your life as your reality becomes blissful.

Mystical things start happening. Moments of synchronicity start happening more and more often. You think of someone and they call you. You buy a book and your teacher tells you, you need go and read such and such book. You have the intuitive feeling you need to be at a specific place at a specific time. At that place you meet a person who connects you to an untapped source of income. These moments of synchronicity have always been there. Meditation has heightened your awareness to the point you become aware of the synchronicity. You clearly recognize these tokens of grace laid out before you. The meditation practice ceases the mechanical way of living in a hurry rushing from experience to experience as you relearn to live in the present moment. Intuition grows and you learn to always listen to that inner voice.

Life eventually becomes a living meditation. Your achievements start to take less effort because your consciousness flows in unison with the Universal Consciousness. Self-forgiveness becomes a reality. The energy of peace and love allow your aura to expand and improve not only your life, but the lives of those around you. Your humility and gentleness make your company more attractive and comforting, yet you continue to remain aware of the ebb and flow of energy within. When your energy starts to wane, you withdraw from the world of the senses and dive into your meditation to recharge with spirit.

It will require a great deal of effort. Spend just a little more time chanting the mantra or whatever your specific meditation practice may be each day. With time and consistency your ability begins to grow. Become the witness and watch for just a little bit longer. Allow yourself to go just a little bit deeper. Night seems darkest just before the dawn. Finally, you break through, and you see the world anew.

8. Samadhi (enlightenment)

A person who seeks out an enlightened master is seeking peace. The true master knows peace in his or her own heart.

God manifests in this world as that sense of peace. Becoming a divine instrument of peace, the enlightened being cultivates peace in the world with every move. When asked how one becomes enlightened, Neem Karoli Baba said the fastest path to enlightenment is, "to serve people and to feed people".

Enlightenment does not come like a big bang all at once. Progressively, over many lifetimes, one traverses the path of the eight limbs. Gradually, throughout this lifetime, you will deepen your experience of truth and enlightenment. Like diving into the ocean, you just keep swimming deeper and deeper.

Becoming enlightened is like receiving a black belt from the Ultimate Guru. The Ultimate Guru is God, and like with any black belt there are degrees. There are degrees to enlightenment. In the earlier degrees, the knowing of the existence of a deeper reality permeates your being. Your real self is not your physical self. During a cross-country drive, you cannot enjoy the view when you are the driver. At some point in your spiritual journey, you decide to let God do the driving and you sit in the passenger seat of life as you enjoy the view. You are not a passive passenger, more God's co-pilot and navigator for the journey. With this perspective of life, you can enjoy the journey even more.

As you gain another degree, your experience deepens. The afflictions of the mind cease. The same way we can train our body to utilize muscle memory, you retrain your mentalmemory. Learning to rejoice in suffering, you come to realize your challenges are blessings. You see all obstacles in life as opportunities to learn and grow. You have trained your brain to instantaneously revert to the meditation or mantra when an issue arises. In this way, each challenge in life actively drives you closer to God.

Next all layers of yourself (koshas) become totally clear. Your true self transparently transmits through your intellect body, emotional body, breath body, and all the way beyond the physical body to manifest as a reality in the material world. Your true self, your spiritual consciousness, physical self and everything in between merge into one complete entity. You cease to exist as God exists exclusively through you. The death of the ego (the individual self) is the birth of eternal life. You return to the source and establish yourself in permanent oneness with the divine. A direct line of communication with God is always available to guide you in His service.

You are not emotionless, rather detached from your emotions. These emotions no longer cloud your decisionmaking ability. Their purpose is realized as motivation to guide those you serve. The master chef gets angry in the kitchen to inspire his assistants to get the job done. The master uses his or her emotions to teach and inspire his students. The spiritual teacher's job is to plant a seed of love in the heart of the aspirant. The great emotional force of the teacher helps to crack the seed and draw its roots in compassion.

Enlightenment is like a thousand-petal lotus that keeps continuously opening into itself. When we learn of the eight limbs, it's like discovering an uncut diamond within ourselves. Practicing the lower limbs is analogous to chipping away at the rock to discover the gem within. Practicing the upper limbs, we use the laser beam of our focus to cut into the core to reveal the diamond of our true self. Attaining enlightenment is the continuous polishing of the gemstone, shining it so it becomes brighter and brighter.

Most people, more than 90 percent of those who claim to be enlightened are not. Someone who is truly enlightened would usually be too humble to call himself a yogi or admit he is enlightened. The enlightened one would be more likely to describe himself or herself as an abhyasi, or a practitioner.

As the Zen saying goes, "Before enlightenment, I chopped wood and carried water, after enlightenment, I chopped wood and carried water". A true master may do things that seem odd and even impure from a lower point of view. You come to a place of knowing or understanding by listening to your intuition.

Enlightenment is learning to live by the seat of your intuition, to follow the heart, to surrender yourself to the Universal will, and dedicate life in ultimate service of the world.

Part 3:

Modern Enlightenment

Chapter 13: Enlightenment for Contemporary Life

Imagine possessing the ability to bless the life of every person you meet. You have this innate capability. It is all a matter of training yourself to operate in the world with your focus always aimed toward your highest intention. Modern enlightenment is simple. It is like becoming a drop of water in the ocean. You recognize yourself as part of a much larger whole and in so doing you are better able to achieve your unique individual purpose. This is not knowledge that comes from me, but universal wisdom that is accessible by all. There are few words to describe the experience of enlightenment.

An understanding of the definition of enlightenment lies in a state of maintained heightened awareness. On the journey, you may experience moments of bliss. True enlightenment is being able to see through the lens of reality indefinitely. It is to be a channel for the divine in every breath, thought, and action. Things that once used to annoy you now lend themselves as guides for your growth and service to others. Gratitude becomes familiar, a way of life, as your understanding of the whole guides you to know the unity in all things.

The divine energy flows through you like the unstoppable current of the river of consciousness. As you become like a drop of water as you flow with this river until you merge into the ocean of love. Surrender to the pull of your heart, like the planets surrender to the universal guidance of gravity. Allow yourself to be blessed and to bless the world. Be compassionate by, instead of creating more attachment, living in a reality based on love. It is true that you should love your neighbor as yourself as Christ taught in the Bible. I encourage you to explore what it means to fall in love with yourself. You will understand that love is what the world needs, not what the ego desires. Meditate on this. Real love is what you need, not what you want.

When you are enlightened, you will see the perfection in all imperfection. Tearing open the veil disintegrates the mechanism creating the illusion of separation. It has been said, to become enlightened, you must want for God like a drowning man wants for air. And when the air comes, it brings with it a burst of fresh energy. Everyone thinks enlightenment comes like a flash, which it can, but more often comes subtly, little by little over a lifetime or many lifetimes. First, you experience small glimpses of nirvana, moments of unexplainable beauty and understanding. These moments are not long lasting, but with patience and consistent practice of Kriya Yoga (daily practice, self-study, and surrender) these moments lengthen in duration and become more frequent. As your meditation deepens, your experience of truth and reality clarifies. Words will always fall short of a true description of enlightenment. Yogi Ji beautifully described Samadhi as the continuous unfolding of a thousandpetal lotus. Think of the experience and feeling of living such beautiful imagery.

Shining enough light on anything makes it beautiful. Enlightenment manifested in the real world is being able to see the beauty in all things. It is to see the harmony between the positive and negative, recognizing the unity and codependence in all. I will give you an example to comprehend this idea. If you were to meet a man who was a convicted felon and known for causing great harm to others, how would you react internally? What impressions would you create even before speaking to the man? The enlightened being would think to himself, "This man has so much potential for greatness. How can I help him in his journey toward transformation? How can I help him achieve his purpose?" He would not have to send the felon love, because he projects an aura of love that already encompasses everyone in his presence.

Imagine living a life of service in a way that seems the most attractive to you. What is your heart calling you to accomplish? Take the ego out of the equation. Forget about money, fame, and power, even the most basic elements of survival. Know that God always has and will always continue to care for your well-being. Start living that life today and let the universe figure out the details. This is living a life of purpose. Learn to live not only with God in your heart but also with your whole heart in God.

The idea of modern enlightenment is somewhat paradoxical. Enlightenment does not change throughout the ages. Although, the way it looks in the modern age is different from earlier times. Not only is the technology different in the contemporary world, our collective value system is highly superficial. Our age is one infatuated with materialism like none other in recorded history. It is time to collectively return to the source and in so doing return to reality.

The yogis of old and some practitioners today are renunciants. Aesthetics who practice their austerities in seclusion have found a sure-fire method to attain enlightenment. Today, renunciation is neither practical for most nor beneficial to the greater good. To renounce all vibrations of pleasure is an admirable path but it truly is the easy path. It requires much more courage and insight to navigate the world in an enlightened state than to hide in seclusion. Live like Christ taught, to be in world but not of it. By this he meant to live in the material without surrendering your influence to anything but that which is divine in nature.

Maintaining such heightened levels of awareness in the modern world requires unprecedented levels of balance. You must pay very close attention to the momentary fluctuations of levels of spirituality in your life. When you are fully charged with spirit go out and share the bounty of your bliss with the world. While you do so, pay close attention to the level of peace you are experiencing. When a person or situation starts to drain your energy, withdraw and return to the sacred space of your meditation. With practice, you will learn what circumstances maintain, raise, and lower your energy. Spending time with likeminded individuals will help you to maintain your peace. When I moved to Encinitas near Paramahansa Yogananda's Self Realization Fellowship, living a spiritual life became much easier. One day, I realized every thought and conversation was about God, spirituality, yoga or something of the like. This led to all my actions being in service of God instead of the small self.

Meditation raises your levels of awareness. Materialism lowers your level of awareness. Learn to recognize these situations in your life. Eventually, you will learn to avoid draining situations and gravitate toward circumstances that maintain and raise the levels of spirit and love in your life. Journaling is a great tool to help heighten your awareness of such situations.

It is not an easy thing to describe enlightenment. If you were to describe eating a mango, what would you say? "It tastes sweet. The texture is soft. I like the taste of the mango. Its flavor is cool and refreshing." Do any of these descriptions fully and completely describe the taste of the mango? Absolutely not. It is impossible to describe how great a mango tastes. If our language lacks the words to accurately describe the taste of a mango, how could it possibly describe a heightened state of awareness like enlightenment? Words will always fall short. The best way to really know is to find out for yourself through your spiritual practice.

Another way to think of enlightenment is a child making the transition from crawling to walking. Once the child begins to walk, he or she will never go back to crawling. Once the child starts walking he or she will probably be running so fast that we can hardly keep up. This is true of enlightenment. Once you know, you will never go back. When a person eats garlic, every word they speak is reminiscent of the smell of garlic. They cannot get away from the smell. So, too, with the enlightened, every word uttered is reminiscent of the divine.

In the next few chapters of the book I will take portions of teachings of a few of the great spiritual masters as a basis for describing the context of modern enlightenment. I take one small portion of a teaching from Krishna of Vrindavan, Siddhartha the Buddha, and Jesus of Nazareth. It is usually easiest to not reinvent the wheel. This modern analysis of the teachings of these ancient masters is my humble attempt to make the truth and relevance of their teachings more accessible to the contemporary spiritual aspirant.

Chapter 14: Krishna and the Bhagavad Gita

The Bhagavad Gita (meaning "The Song of God") is a dialogue between Krishna and Arjuna. The Gita is a piece in a much larger story named the Mahabharata (which means "The Great War"). Krishna is a divine incarnation and Arjuna is a warrior whose duty has led him and his country to the brink of imminent civil war. The story begins in a chariot as the pair overlooks the battlefield. Arjuna collapses, as he is overwhelmed with grief and fear. He cannot go on with his duty. To him, it seems better to turn and run than to fight with his own countrymen, friends, teachers, family, and even his own grandfather. In his infinite wisdom, Krishna gives Arjuna the ultimate pep talk cultivating the strength in Arjuna's heart to rise to his destiny. I recommend everyone take the time to study this epic transmission of ancient wisdom and to practice applying its guidance to modern living. Gandhi read the Gita daily and attributed the satyagraha (non-violence) movement to his interpretation and embodiment of its teachings.

Regarding enlightenment, Arjuna asks how he can recognize wisdom and Krishna responds with the ultimate truth. The translation provided here is from Eknath Easwaran's, "Essence of the Bhagavad Gita"

Arjuna: Tell me of those who live established in wisdom ever aware of the self, O Krishna, how do they talk? How sit? How move about?

Krishna: They live in wisdom who see themselves in all and all in them, who have renounced every selfish desire and sense craving tormenting the heart. Neither agitated by grief or hankering from pleasure, they live free from lust and fear and anger. Established in meditation, they are truly wise. Fettered no more by self-attachments, they are neither elated by good fortune nor depressed by bad. Such are the seers.

What does an enlightened person look like in a contemporary setting? How would they talk, sit, and move?

When you realize the truth about who you really are, your desires merge with desire of God. In our society, we are constantly bombarded with materialism and consumerism. To overcome these unnatural tendencies, desire for yourself what God wants for you. The yearning for more only creates more suffering. Not all desires create suffering. Desire of the material will inevitably create suffering because material desires can only be temporarily fulfilled. Direct your desire toward the attainment of divine communion because this relationship is eternal. It will not create suffering because it is never-ending.

As you come to an understanding of the unity and truth in all things in nature, the suffering from emotional instability fades away. You come to a state of infinite bliss and innocence through meditation. Rumi wrote, "There is a place beyond the good and the bad. I will meet you there." You will stop clinging to the impermanent when you realize our own miniscule understanding is encompassed by the omnipresent truth. This order guides all movement. Knowing this truth allows you to remain unmoved as your connection to reality is permanent and unchanging.

When you break down the word understanding you have "under" and "standing" or "that which stands under". By placing themselves below the magnificence of the Infinite Knowing, all true seers, yogi's, spiritual masters and the like are humbled and able to surrender to an unbound grace. They are shown the error in the ways of a material man. They recognize that which is temporary and that which is everlasting. They gravitate toward truth and in this manner, they are unaffected by the winds of change, like all other mortal men. The wise become immortal by means of God-identification obtained through the practice of meditation.

Krishna: Even as a tortoise draws in its limbs, the wise draw in their senses at will. Aspirants abstain from sense pleasures but they still crave for them. These cravings all disappear when they see the highest goal. Even of those who tread the path, the stormy senses can sweep off the mind. They live in wisdom who subdue their senses and keep their mind ever absorbed in me.

Meditation is key. In meditation, we learn to control our senses like reins control a raging stallion. In meditation exists the ability to turn from external sensory stimulation to internal sensory stimulation. Meditation gives you the ability to monitor and increase the level of your spiritual energy. When you notice your energy getting low, like the tortoise, withdraw your awareness inward. In the inner realm, recharge from your naturally built in divine power outlet. This is a crucial skill in our world today overloaded with advertisements at every turn.

Being enticed by physical pleasure enslaves consciousness in the realm of the impermanent. It is perfectly fine to enjoy pleasures of the world, but thinking happiness comes from sensory stimulation is a fallacy. Even spiritual seekers can get caught in the bright lights of Las Vegas. When you glimpse the light of awareness in your true self, sincerity for the path becomes your anchor to weather any storm. Those who have seen truth, who have drunk from the cup of reality, focus all their energy on uniting with God. As the nature of the sponge is to soak up water, your nature is to be absorbed into the heart of God.

Krishna: When you keep thinking about sense objects attachment comes. Attachment breeds desire, the lust of possession that burns to anger. Anger clouds judgment. You can no longer learn from past mistakes. Lost is the power to choose between what is wise and what is unwise and your life

is utter waste. But when you move amidst the world of the senses free from attachment and aversion alike, there comes the peace in which all sorrows end and you live in the wisdom of the self.

When the focus of life becomes attaining material possessions (clothes, cars, money, sex, a certain lifestyle), you become attached to your materialism. For most in Western society, materialism has become a religion. It is really a virus that is very easily contracted. In your own mind, it defines who you are. Materialism creates an artificial need for more. The fact that we will never be able to satisfy the mind's endless wanting creates frustration, anger, and discontent. You lose the ability to discern and no longer function from dimensions of the heart. You can ascend the kleshas, the five afflictions of the mind (ignorance, ego, attachment, aversion, and fear) through daily spiritual practice, introspection, and surrender to the divine will (Kriya Yoga). Even today, through this practice you can experience the peace of the unconditioned mind, enlightenment.

Attachment creates the disease of wanting more. This disease is progressive in stages: attachment, desire, lust, and finally anger. When we give in to low energy emotions like anger, we lose the ability to be discerning and have no chance of achieving any meaningful purpose in life. Krishna describes this state as a life wasted. Why does man care so much about pleasing the ego of other men? A person wants a nice car to impress people he does not even know as he drives on the freeway. It is much more important to earn the approval of God. You do not earn His approval by having lots of money or owning fancy things; earn Divine approval through the attainment of spiritual principals. When God holds you in high esteem, no material goods can even come close to the blessing He will bestow on you.

Krishna: The disunited mind is far from wise; how can it meditate? How be at peace? When you know no peace, how can you know joy? When you let your mind follow the call of the senses, they carry away your better judgment as storms drive a boat off its charted course on the sea.

The mind can be compared to a lake during a storm. The surface of the lake is our conscious mind, that which we can control. Below the surface is the subconscious including our fears and desires. The storm churns the emotional water so we cannot see through to the bottom of the lake. Meditation stills the conscious mind, giving us the opportunity for introspection of the subconscious and a means to overcome unsubstantiated fears and desires.

When you lose the ability to focus your mind, you cease to operate at your maximum potential. Meditation is creating an intense laser beam focus. Such a focus is a prerequisite for creating and maintaining the tranquil space required by peace. To experience happiness, you must be at peace in your own heart. You must accept and be content with your situation in life. You may not have as much or all the material possessions you might like, but instead choose to direct your focus on gratitude for that which you have been blessed with.

When the material world misdirects your attention away from reality, you lose the ability to discern. Just as rush hour traffic slows to a halt, in materialism your spiritual evolution ceases to progress. When you notice this happening, redirect your energy. As soon as possible dive back in to your spiritual practice. Maybe all you need to do to reorient your attention is repeat the mantra (saying the name of God) silently to yourself for a moment. Shift your focus from the worldly to the Godly and divine communion again becomes possible.

Krishna: Use all your power to free the senses from attachment and aversion alike and live in the full wisdom on

the Self. Such a sage awakens light in the night of all creatures. That which the world calls day is the night of ignorance to the wise.

Becomes your own hero. Practice heroically. Do not try to have a great meditation. It is more important to make your spiritual practice a steady one. A consistent effort is a heroic spiritual effort. It is not a challenge to come to do a spiritual practice one single time. True devotion is returning to your practice day in and day out, especially when you do not feel like it. You must become devoted to devotion. This consistency gives you the opportunity to analyze your thought process with equanimity and detach from your likes and dislikes. Such a modus operandi creates an understanding and sense of purpose in your life.

The modern world lives in a perpetual state of darkness (ignorance). The mind is clouded by conditioned existence. This conditioning causes us to be ignorant of reality. Your sadhana (daily spiritual practice) cultivates a fire in you. The product of your spiritual fire is the perpetual light of awareness. This light allows you to see the entirety of a situation when everyone else is blind to reality. Freedom from your own affinities empowers you to live with purpose and in the service of others. Realizing this light, you become a conduit for truth as the wisdom of the ages permeates through you.

From maintaining a mentality of separation, we live in darkness. Living in unity with the divine diffuses light through every aspect of our being. In our nature, we are light beings. Lifting the veil of separation uncovers the truth of the self.

On the planet, there is both a light and dark side because the sun can only illuminate one half of the planet at a time. Regardless of this fact, the sun is always shining throughout space and time. It is the same with the light of God. If you choose to only recognize the living reality of the divine half of the time, it does not mean God has forsaken you. The wise choose to see Him in every moment and in everything.

Krishna: As rivers flow into the ocean but cannot make the vast ocean overflow, so flow the streams of the sense world into the sea of peace that is the sage. But this is not so with the desirer of desires.

Peace is entirely abundant in the universe encompassing all things. To tune into this peace, one must tune out of the world of the physical senses. Meditation is the metronome to harmonize our vibration with the empowering vibration of serenity. One who has realized the self understands that truth lies within. We are not meant to be slaves to our senses, but rather their master. We can only make this paradigm shift when we consciously choose to do so. In a meditative state of tranquility, you can discerningly interpret the information coming in from the senses. When you are in control of the senses, you affect the world instead of allowing the world to infect you. Choose to create peace in the world, instead of allowing the world to create emotional instability in you.

One controlled by the senses has no control over desire. Eknath Easwaran explained, "There is much more satisfaction in resisting wrong desire than yielding to it". Through meditation, you regain control of your consciousness and swallow the sense world making it as powerless as a placebo. were powerless like a placebo. Because you recognize the sense world for what it is, you avoid all its negative side effects.

Krishna: They are forever free who renounce all selfish desires and break away from the ego cage of "I", "me", and "mine" to unite with the Lord. This is the supreme state. Attain to this and pass from death to immortality.

Jesus said, "What does a man get if he loses his soul but gains the world?" To find your soul, you must lose your self. In this context, self means identification with the ego. St. Francis describes this evolution saying, "In dying to the self, we are born to eternal life".

For those of the material world, success is gratification of the ego. For those harmonized with spirit, success is bliss or enlightenment. Ego gratification, if attainable, can only be temporary. It is possible to harmonize your vibration with the divine and maintain this balance eternally. Bliss is the ability to find the extraordinary in the ordinary. Dr. Wayne Dyer gave a statement perfect for this moment, "Enlightenment is your ego's biggest disappointment."

To those closest to him, Buddha was a failure. His father, wife, advisors all thought he had lost his mind. According to them, leaving a princely life for the life of an aesthetic was the biggest mistake he could have made. Because he tasted truth and knew it existed, none of this mattered. Buddha was not trying to impress anyone else or satisfy his ego. What he was after was much deeper satisfaction of the soul. Meditation is what guided him there, and it is what will guide you there also.

Even if we are successful at impressing others by our possessions, it will not make us happy. Enlightenment is the goal, divine union. Aim for the target and you will hit the bulls eye. When you connect to bliss through meditation, you let go of the impermanent and connect to what is permanent and eternal in you.

Chapter 15: Buddha and the Dhammapada

The following section is my interpretation of the Buddha's teaching describing the wise. The selection is a chapter borrowed from the "The Dhammapada", which is a collection of the Buddha's teachings compiled after his death by devoted students.

The previous chapter in the Dhammapada describes the traits of the immature or childlike. Using the term "childlike" demonstrates the Buddha's understanding that everyone possesses the innate ability to grow, mature and transform spiritually. It has been said that we have two births in this life. The first is when we enter the physical world through the form of the body. The second birth takes place when we awaken to the spiritual world all around us.

By reading this far into the book, you have undoubtedly begun the awakening process and started breathing the mystical air all around you. In Buddhism, there are two terms used to describe the journey to enlightenment. The first is "Bodhi". Bodhi is a temporary instantaneous awakening where the fluctuations of the mind cease momentarily. Dormant realms of consciousness become animated and you receive a taste of what is to come. "Nirvana" is the permanent attainment of this state achieved through continued, consistent, focused effort. You may experience momentary glimpses of your own divine magnificence in the Bodhi mind. Nirvana is complete and total attainment of the enlightened way of living. Awareness becomes constant and uninterrupted. When nirvana is attained, the practitioner has become self-realized, connected to his or her own Christ-consciousness, become a Buddha, and is a living embodiment of the greatest source of truth in the universe.

I present to you here the Chapter of "The Wise" in "The Dhammapada" as translated by Eknath Easwaran.

If you see someone wise, who can steer you away from the wrong path, follow that person as you would one who can reveal hidden treasures. Only good can come of it.

To meet a wise or enlightened being is one of the greatest blessings in existence. The opportunity to learn directly from such a being for a prolonged period of time is yet an even greater blessing. Seize this opportunity and give your entire effort because that which is to be obtained is indescribable. When asked to describe enlightenment, the Buddha encouraged his students that the only way to truly know, was to find out for themselves.

The eagerness and willingness to follow such a person in the beginning can save a seeker much suffering. I say this from experience. You do not truly appreciate what you have until it is gone. There were times in my life when I did not take full advantage of the guidance of my teachers. Only in their absence was I able to totally value the treasure of their wisdom. The time away from my teachers was like living in the unconscious agony of darkness. A yearning to receive their love developed in my heart. Instantly, in one moment, I realized my Guru's love has been and will always be guiding me toward the light.

Seize every opportunity you have to learn from the wise. Take full advantage of this blessing. All encounters in life are but fleeting and temporary. Appreciate, recognize, and honor your teachers. Their service is of the Highest. May you, too, be blessed to follow in their footsteps one day.

Let them admonish or instruct or restrain you from what is wrong. They will be loved by the good but disliked by the bad.

You may be initiated to study through a spiritual teacher in a formal or informal process. The initiation process is meant to heighten the meaning of the experience and increase the level of importance you put on the divine transaction taking place. If you pay a small price for an article of clothing, the cloth will always be cheap to you. If the clothes were expensive, you would value them because of their great cost. So, too, is it with this spiritual affair I am describing. If you put little into the process, it could be money, effort, importance, devotion, or anything else you value, you will in return receive little value from the lesson.

When you value your teacher's guidance, you are more likely to "let them admonish or instruct or restrain you" on the spiritual path. When beginning to live the spiritual life, most do not understand the relevance in many of the ritual practices performed and taught by their masters. In the beginning, I thought these practices were only habitual and held little meaning. Over time, I began to recognize the value of my meditation teacher, and appreciate the wealth of wisdom he could know only from his remarkable vantage point. I eventually learned all the rituals he taught served to consecrate the meditation space and practice itself.

I began to allow my teacher to caution me on things that hindered my progress, the quality of my practice improved tremendously. Listening to his instruction, I could reap the full benefit of the practice. Allowing him to restrain me from certain bad habits (for example restraining me from eating meat), I eliminated all obstructions so I could obtain the goal.

When I introduced spiritually aligned, truth-seeking people to my teacher, they fell in love with and became devoted to him. When I introduced someone worldly and materialistic to my Guru, the person held him in great disdain, and spoke poorly of him slandering his name. This happened because the spiritually awake can recognize a person with elevated consciousness for who he or she is. Those living a conditioned existence under the control of the ego are insulted when they see or hear the truth. They do not see the Guru for who He truly is.

The Hanuman Chalisa is an ancient Hindu song written in the Pali language. The beginning of the song translates, "Taking the dust from the lotus feet of the Guru, I polish the mirror of my heart." A real spiritual guide reflects a clear reflection of who you really are, past all the layers of conditioning. Those controlled by the ego dislike this reflection because this awakening eventually leads to the death of the ego. The experience is uncomfortable for them. Growth is always uncomfortable in some way or another. Humble ones devote themselves to such a teacher as they recognize him or her as a guide on the path to truth.

Christ taught, "The meek shall inherit the earth". The meek are humble. The humble are those who evolve and ascend beyond the ego. Humility allows one to keep the glass empty so the teacher can fill it. They take advice and learn from the wise. Devotion to the Guru opens the door to the heart. Surrender allows you to cross the threshold, which unveils a completely new world.

Make friends with those who are good and true, not with those who are bad and false.

Jesus, Buddha, and Krishna all dispense similar advice to us in more topics than one. This fact proves the existence of a universal truth. Searching for an understanding and practicing this truth is an important way to stick to the spiritual path.

Keeping the company of honest, righteous, spiritually aligned individuals allows one to deepen devotion and develop similar characteristics. The energy of others influences us just as our energy influences them. Maintaining unrighteous, dishonest company encourages the belief that such traits are satisfactory. The energy of such individuals is cumbersome and draining. Be discerning about who you spend the most time with. The five people in the world who you spend the most time with have the greatest effect on your personality. Think of who these people are in your life. Perhaps you could benefit by spending more or less time with certain people. In this manner, you help those who need your influence by spending time with them until they begin to drain you physically, emotionally, and spiritually. Stay inspired by devoting more time to those who positively influence you as they will uplift rather than drain your heart and soul. Do your best to surround yourself with others who are on the same path as you. This is also important advice for cultivating romantic relationships that encourage your spiritual evolution.

Choose to totally avoid those negative, intolerant few who bring you down and make you doubt your own calling. Take advantage of spending time with the pure and true as you will benefit from the empowerment they reflect in you. Also, remember spending time alone is the best way to recharge in your own sense of Presence. Valuing time alone allows you to have a greater appreciation for spending time with others.

To follow the dharma revealed by the noble ones is to live in joy with a serene mind.

In Buddhism, the term "dharma" represents the way or the teachings of Buddha. "Dharma" in Sanskrit or "dhamma" in Pali refers to duty, laws, righteousness, order, and purpose. There is no noble and higher path to follow one's duty, to recognize the way, to live in purpose. Spiritual teachers guide the seeker to realize their purpose. This path can only be achieved by living with awareness in the present moment. Suffering exists in the past and future. Staying grounded to purpose by remaining in the present moment is the way to circumvent all suffering and experience peace.

A person possesses both an inner and outer dharma, or purpose. The inner purpose is universal to all, to realize the divine within. The outer purpose is unique and emanates from the inner purpose. The outer purpose is manifesting God's will in the world by living consciously in the present moment.

Instead of focusing on an outer purpose being some overwhelming duty, task, or accomplishment, one must develop in life a focus on just being. Bringing attention to the present moment allows us to experience the expansive peace of beingness. By staying conscious in the present moment, we dedicate all our energy to the here and now. Taking one step at a time, an athlete can complete a marathon. So, in taking each step of life while staying in the present moment, we string together an infinite number of individual moments in the present creating a serene, meaningful, purpose-filled life.

The inner purpose is to know God. The outer purpose is manifesting God. The path to both is through heightened awareness of our inherent Presence. Presence is peace. God is peace. Self-realization is the discovery of peace within. It is like striking gold, finding something you never knew existed subtly hidden inside you all along. Respecting the guidance of the knowers, the seeker makes known the ultimate truth and finds peace in attaining life's purpose.

As irrigators lead water where they want, as archers make their arrows straight, as carpenters carve wood, the wise shape their minds.

In my opinion this is one of the most beautiful verses in the whole Dhammapada if not all of antiquity. The author's use of metaphor is excellent and imparts a clear vision of how the wise overcome mental conditioning. Dividing and contemplating this passage unveils great insights into mastery of the mind.

One who has mastered the art of irrigation knows exactly how to guide water to the parts of a field that need it the most. In the same way, the enlightened know what to avoid and spend time doing what is needed to maintain their energy. The master irrigator utilizes the best and most efficient method to water a field. In the same manner, the master of meditation knows the most effective and efficient methods of meditation to use to train the mind.

Archers make their arrows straight so that when they loosen the projectile from their bow, they will find the mark. So, too, do wise ones prepare a seat for spiritual practice that allows their effort to remain concentrated and undisturbed that they may accomplish their goals. The practice is preformed consistently at the same time daily, which increases the accuracy and effectiveness of the ritual.

A great carpenter chooses and prepares the best piece of wood to he what he needs to create a masterpiece. He painstakingly whittles out each imperfection until achieving an unprecedented level of excellence. The spiritual aspirant prepares his or her mind with the proper stimulation, avoiding violent entertainment, reading spiritual literature, and maintaining the proper diet to create a healthy life. The aspirant chooses the best company to keep to remain motivated and on course. In the meditation practice, the aspirant painstakingly carves out mental imperfections created by the constant bombardment of conditioning so that can be overcome.

In mastering their art, the irrigator, the archer, the carpenter, and the meditator apply the appropriate effort and the appropriate surrender in each situation that presents itself. These skills can only be perfected with awareness in the present moment. The irrigator, archer, and carpenter must devote total focus to the task at hand. With an intense concentration, the spiritual aspirant becomes a craftsman creating a steady mind devoid of ego, disturbed by nothing, unveiling the wisdom of the unconditioned reality.

As a solid rock cannot be moved by the wind, the wise are not shaken by praise or blame. When they listen to the words of the dharma, their minds become calm and clear like the waters of a still lake.

The wise are beyond the influences of the good and bad. They are unmoved by impermanent occurrences in the world. It is the ego that judges, separates, and fragments life from the entirety of the whole creating the individual self. This theme recurs constantly throughout ancient literature especially in the Bhagavad Gita and the Dhammapada.

Ramana Maharishi explains, "When the mind comes out of the Self, the world appears. Therefore, when the world appears (to be real), the Self does not appear; and when the Self appears (shines) the world does not appear."

The physical world as we interpret it is an illusion of the mind. The Celestial Self is the true reality of God. Before incarnating into an earthly existence all beings are in union with the divine. The moment of material conception the mind is born, the illusion is created, and the veil of ignorance begins to hide the truth. By mastering meditation or another form of spiritual practice, the small self or the individual "I" dissolves into the big Self.

The ego is a creation of the mind. It is what judges and blames. The ego labels something as good or bad, right or wrong, full of praise or fault, and it lusts or hates. In meditation, we learn to kill the ego and rediscover the Self. In the realm of the Self, love, peace, and harmony flow ceaselessly through all things. Because the spiritual being is not enslaved by the mental processes labeling thoughts with different judgments and opinions, the mental process comes to a standstill. The waters of the mind become serene. The truth is seen clearly as it radiates through every layer of existence. The enlightened have withdrawn the mind back to the Self. Light energizes, permeates, and connects all. At this point, instead of separating, perception unites.

Acceptance is the most important modality for coming to a place of equanimity. The willingness to receive a situation as it is, facilitates equal-mindedness and allows a person to remain unmoved by external circumstances. Acceptance makes way for enjoyment and ultimately enthusiasm for life.

Good people keep on walking whatever happens. They do not speak vain words and are the same in good fortune and bad. If one desires neither children nor power nor success by unfair means, know such a one to be good, wise, and virtuous.

The enlightened accept their plight without judgment. They are past the point of merely believing in the necessity of suffering. They are even past the point of knowing there is a reason behind each obstacle. The wise have come to the realization that every situation encountered in life relates to a greater purpose and embrace the circumstance. With this state of mind, gratitude and humility arise allowing one to overcome every hurdle with an indomitable will. This is real power! When one resolves to hold the course and never give up for any reason, quitting ceases to even hold a space in the mind. With this mentality, success is inevitable. One embraces suffering recognizing it is an appropriate means to an admirable ending.

The wise hold their tongue often and refrain from saying what does not need to be said. Those who over speak waste much energy. The effectiveness of speech improves with an increase of contemplation and by not allowing oneself to be controlled by the ego. Surpassing the threshold of the ego creates the space for acceptance, which leads to equanimity, peace of mind, and connection to the heart.

The process of labeling things as good or bad loses all importance. The sense of calm experienced in the present moment overcomes all illusions prompted by past regrets or future fears. Instead of striving for the attainment of material desires, the enlightened mind surrenders to the divine will and places a greater emphasis on spiritual desire.

Few are those who reach the other shore; most people keep running up and down this shore. But those who follow the

dharma, when it has been well taught, will reach the other shore, hard to reach beyond the power of death.

In this wonderful analogy, the Buddha describes the journey to enlightenment. The near shore represents the conditioned state of existence, the state an overwhelming majority of people identifies with. The river represents the torrent of consciousness, running wild with the energy to sweep away all but the strongest of swimmers. Dharma is following the righteous path. It is recognizing a duty or purpose in life and staying true to the course. In the analogy, following dharma is knowing how to swim. Those who are fluent in the teaching of dharma, those who know how to swim well, make it to the other shore.

Knowledge and its application are two very different realities. It is one thing to recognize your dharma, duty, or purpose. It is an entirely different reality to live your purpose. Even when it is challenging, when you become busy, caught up in emotions, frustrated, hungry, tired, lose faith, or fall under the grip of any other conditioned modality, you must stay true to the course. It is rare to find someone with this ability. This power comes through correct identification, by knowing the truth, staying rooted in the essential Self.

A good teacher guides you to this point by encouraging consistent spiritual practice, introspection and surrender. Mastering these methods will allow you to navigate your way across the river to an unconditioned existence, to enlightenment. You must be compassionate to yourself and ever persistent while learning to swim across the stream of consciousness, this river of reality; the tributary of truth. By the time you have made it to the other shore, you will have cultivated the strength and gained the knowledge necessary to make the journey back and forth and remain in a state of equanimity unaffected by the torrent of perception. You will have connected to your Eternal Self, your God-consciousness. This is the part of you that is everlasting and never dies.

The far shore is the state of enlightenment. Over time, gradually, you will learn the subtle techniques needed to reach and remain on the far shore, where the grass is always greenest, where the lotus flower of the heart is always in full bloom.

They leave darkness behind and follow the light. They give up home and leave pleasure behind. Calling nothing their own, they purify their hearts and rejoice. Well trained in the seven fields of enlightenment, their senses disciplined and free from attachments, they live in freedom full of light.

Whether it is day or night on the planet earth, the sun always shines throughout the universe. If it is the night on your place in the planet, sunlight still makes its way to you via the reflection off the moon. The Self and the mind function by the same means. The mind is analogous with the moon and the Self is the Sun or the light of awareness.

When an individual is awake, or fully conscious, the light of Self shines undistorted. In the night of ignorance, the mind is the moon reflecting the light of the Self. Although the mind functions unconsciously, it operates as a reflection of the divine manifesting the light of the Self. As perception improves, the quality of the light clarifies until eventually night becomes day and the Self is perceived directly.

In this metaphor night becomes day by letting go of the attachment to night or unconscious conditioned living. You do not have to give up your home and leave behind all worldly pleasure. It is necessary to give up the attachment to home and worldly pleasure as they will never give happiness. Understand that happiness comes from within as happiness is the Self. Nobody really owns anything indefinitely. All things in the physical world are impermanent. The clothes you wear, the house you live in, the car you drive, even your spouse and family are all momentary relationships, not examples of indefinite ownership. As we let go of our attachment to things and recognize their impermanence, we can enjoy them for what they are and appreciate them even more. As perception clears, the heart becomes lighter. Contentment and joyousness become reality as the night of ignorance transforms to the day of complete consciousness.

The seven fields of enlightenment are: mindfulness, vigor, joy, serenity, concentration, equanimity, and the penetration of dharma (the ability to see universal order in all processes of life). Mindfulness is an echelon of consciousness in all actions. Vigor refers to maintaining a youthful vibrant mentality so that you may manifest this playful energy physically. Joy is the permeation of happiness in your life. Serenity is to know the peace of the divine in each moment. Concentration denotes the ability to create the mental state of intense focus such as that experienced in meditation. Equanimity is a stance of equal-mindedness. It is a recognition of the unity in all life, an appreciation for the equality in all. The penetration of dharma is an understanding that purpose exists in every circumstance. Each moment guides you toward your destiny.

Cultivating a sense of mastery in these fields through devoted practice releases the bondage of attachment and allows the light of the Self to permeate all levels of awareness. Freedom or enlightenment becomes a reality.

This sums up Buddha's teaching of the wise. He makes several points that are interwoven with the truth highlighted by both Krishna and Christ. Revere a qualified teacher by following their instruction. Surround yourself with an uplifting inner circle. Follow the righteous path by living purposefully and adhering to your duty. Train the mind to be steady beyond all external influences. Let nothing dissuade you from your path or disturb your peace. Attain freedom by giving up attachments. This may appear to be a tall order, but by following the methods of the Buddha, enlightenment is entirely attainable.

Chapter 16: Jesus and the Sermon on the Mount

The full spectrum of the teachings of Jesus Christ can be understood through a study of his sermon on the mount. I recommend all who are interested study this gospel in its entirety located in the book of Matthew in the Bible from chapters five through seven. The gospel will be divided into sections as we discuss the timeless teachings of Christ. I will label each section with its coordinating verse so you can read each portion before the interpretation. There is an incredible wealth of wisdom to be gained from the study of this sermon. I again encourage you to read and reread the passage as you interpret the relevance of its universal truths in your life.

A crowd gathered and Jesus the Christ readied to bestow the blessing of his discourse. The seekers sat with great excitement and anticipation to hear the words of the enlightened master.

The Beatitudes 5:1-12

Seeing the crowds, he went up on the mountain, and when he sat down, his disciples came to him. And he opened his mouth and taught them, saying, "Blessed are the poor in spirit, for theirs is the kingdom of heaven. Blessed are those who mourn, for they shall be comforted. Blessed are the meek, for they shall inherit the earth. Blessed are those who hunger and thirst for righteousness, for they shall be satisfied. Blessed are the merciful, for they shall receive mercy. Blessed are the pure in heart, for they shall see God. are the peacemakers, for they shall be called sons of God. Blessed are those who are persecuted for righteousness' sake, for theirs is the kingdom of heaven. Blessed are you when others revile you and persecute you and utter all kinds of evil against you falsely on my

account. Rejoice and be glad, for your reward is great in heaven, for so they persecuted the prophets who were before you.

Jesus begins his sermon by blessing the poor, those in mourning, the humble, the hungry, those in search of truth and righteousness, the merciful, the pure, the peaceful, and the persecuted. He promises them they will find their own heaven. God answers our prayers in the way we need him to, not necessarily the way we want Him too. Remember, real love is what we need, not what we want. Heaven and hell exist in the here and now; they are determined by our interpretation of reality. Be grateful for the challenges you are presented. Those challenges are what inspire your personal and spiritual evolution. This is the same way all great beings attained such heights.

Do not pay attention to, dwell upon, or even respond to those who lie, mock, or treat you badly. Dealing with challenging people is an opportunity to practice and develop compassion for them and for yourself. Cultivate a sense of appreciation and sympathy for these people. Without them growth would be impossible. Think about Tobias Lars' statement, "The maggots and leeches in your life have a huge purpose in bringing life back into your soul and your awareness and awake-ness and discrimination." Alternative healing practices utilize maggots to eat away the dead flesh from a wound and leeches to suck out infected blood. Detaching from challenging people is an incredibly powerful process of realigning our soul with its purpose.

Understand that these difficult people are in a different place in their journeys. You have been where they are, and by learning from your example one day they may be where you are. Everyone goes through their own process. Here in the Beatitudes Christ states, "Be happy about it. Be very glad! For a great reward awaits you in heaven." Heaven is within. Dig deep in your own psyche to find the opportunities in your obstacles.

Salt and Light 5:13-16

You are the salt of the earth, but if salt has lost its taste, how shall its saltiness be restored? It is no longer good for anything except to be thrown out and trampled under people's feet.

You are the light of the world. A city set on a hill cannot be hidden. Nor do people light a lamp and put it under a basket, but on a stand, and it gives light to all in the house. In the same way, let your light shine before others, so that they may see your good works and give glory to your Father who is in heaven.

Unless you stay inspired, your life becomes ineffective and joyless. Maintaining motivation allows you put the best step of your best self forward in every stride. When that sense of excitement ceases, life becomes as if it were "worthless". Living a life worth living, following purpose, serving others by fulfilling your destiny means keeping the salt of life full of flavor.

Devote time to yourself by doing activities that kindle inspiration. The juiciest orange has the most flavor. A few examples of how to keep life juicy are spending time in nature, gong on a hike, taking a long swim in the ocean, spending a night camping out under the stars or doing any other outdoor activity that appeals to you. Taking ample Vitamin N (nature) ensures our lives are infused with genuine humanity. Sometimes all we need to do is change up the routine and stop living so mechanically.

I cannot forget to say that serving others is one of the best ways to cultivate inspiration. By serving and teaching others, we get to witness firsthand their revelatory experiences and in turn remember and relive the experiences that changed our own lives. Whenever I teach workshops and help others discover their truths within, I come to a deeper level of understanding the truth within my own heart and I find inspiration to keep going deeper down that path. Experiencing the love that outpours from service is incredibly empowering and energizing.

Explore some of your childhood activities. When you reconnect to your roots, your inner light permeates from the deepest level of your soul, past the intellect, emotions, the breath body, and the physical body to illuminate the world. The light represents unbound awareness, supreme consciousness. Darkness cannot exist in the presence of light. Why would we ever want to cover the light of our true self with materialism or ego? When we remove all obstructions from the light, we access Christ-consciousness, Buddhahood, salvation, the Toa, enlightenment or whatever you choose to term the highest aspect of yourself. That aspect is your divine element. You contain "the light of the world…that cannot be hidden". When you live through your essential nature, the celestial materializes in the physical realm. Remember, you are here as a representative of God, act accordingly. When you earn accolades and recognition, it is God acknowledged through you. Give credit where credit is due and honor Him.

Law 5:17-20

Do not think that I have come to abolish the Law or the Prophets; I have not come to abolish them but to fulfill them. For truly, I say to you, until heaven and earth pass away, not an iota, not a dot, will pass from the Law until all is accomplished. Therefore, whoever relaxes one of the least of these commandments and teaches others to do the same will be called least in the kingdom of heaven, but whoever does them and teaches them will be called great in the kingdom of heaven. For I tell you, unless your righteousness exceeds that of the scribes and Pharisees, you will never enter the kingdom of heaven.

The spiritual aspirant seeks a way to live the middle path following both God's law and man's law. Although, the divine order supersedes man's laws, both sets of regulations can be used to guide us toward righteousness and order. The sets of principles are not always in agreement, but there is always a middle path to be taken. In the 22nd chapter of Matthew the Pharisees use a lawyer to trick Christ. The lawyer asked Jesus if citizens can get out of paying taxes because His kingdom is not of this world, Jesus responded, "Give back to Caesar what is Caesar's and give to the God what belongs to God". Christ's response serves as an excellent example of overcoming the duality of God's and man laws by taking the middle path.

The purpose of following the spiritual path is not to put oneself above the law, rather it is to create a clarity and understanding of the universal truth, which exist and governs all levels of reality. When you discover one of these truths, you find it remains evident in each layer of the self from the physical, the breath, the emotional, the intellect, and the spirit. The truth is the same for the young and the old, the wise and the ignorant, regardless if they recognize it. The fully awakened live truth in every aspect of their existence. Every chakra and the principles they represent, survival, pleasure, power, love, creativity, intuition, and spirit are all fully activated when aligned with the truth.

We must evaluate for ourselves the best way to live the truth. Do not internalize any teaching or suggestion, even from your most regarded teachers without using discernment. One of my martial arts instructors would always say, "Take everything with a grain of salt." What works for someone else might not be true for you. Make righteousness an ideal, the ultimate priority for life. On the freeway of the spiritual journey, living righteously allows us to travel on course without swerving between lanes, orienting toward that which is true instead of false, living in light instead of darkness, enjoying nectar instead of poison.

Anger 5:21-26

You have heard that it was said to those of old, 'You shall not murder; and whoever murders will be liable to judgment.' But I say to you that everyone who is angry with his brother will be liable to judgment; whoever insults his brother will be liable to the council; and whoever says, 'You fool!' will be liable to the hell. So, if you are offering your gift at the altar and there remember that your brother has something against you, leave your gift there before the altar and go. First be reconciled to your brother, and then come and offer your gift. Come to terms quickly with your accuser while you are going with him to court, lest your accuser hand you over to the judge, and the judge to the guard, and you be put in prison. Truly, I say to you, you will never get out until you have paid the last penny.

    This teaching educates us on the uselessness of anger. Unjust anger only compounds an individual's problems and distorts his or her perception of the world. Christ speaks of how murder, anger, insulting others, and cursing are all wrong. When we judge one sin as worse than another, we create levels allowing certain forms of evil to be more acceptable than others. We do ourselves a great disservice. Right is right and wrong is wrong. To live in alignment with the truth, that which is righteous is the path of the spiritually devoted.

    Examining the Greek word "sin" explains the misinterpretation by which most decipher the term. The true meaning of sin is "to miss the mark". The word derives from archery competition and describes what happens when an archer misses the target entirely. In the context of our actions and behaviors, it connotes living off target or out of alignment with purpose.

In terms of consciousness, the light within us is either on or off. There is no dimmer switch in terms of our mindfulness. We either act in or out of alignment with our purpose. We choose to either live in awareness of the spirit or die in ignorance of the truth. With this understanding, there is no middle ground. All our thoughts, words, and actions should be made as an offering to the Ruler of the earthly and celestial abode.

If something is bothering you before you preform your spiritual practice (meditation, yoga, prayer, silence etc.), correct the misalignment, right the wrong, and then come to your practice. Sometimes when I get emotional, it is better to do some yoga or meditation first so I can come to a clearer perspective on how to handle the problem. What Christ is referring to here is the times we intuitively know something is wrong and exactly what to do to make it right. Remembering sin is living off course, we must align our lives in every opportunity to live a spiritual life and maintain a spiritual practice. In this manner, all actions become devotional. Your life becomes a living, breathing meditation. As soon as you notice yourself sinning, or veering off course, correct your actions, focus your intention, adjust your aim. By this method your existence becomes a dynamic sacrificial offering in service of the Lord.

Relationships 5:27-30

You have heard that it was said, 'You shall not commit adultery.' But I say to you that everyone who looks at a woman with lustful intent has already committed adultery with her in his heart. If your right eye causes you to sin, tear it out and throw it away. For it is better that you lose one of your members than that your whole body be thrown into hell. And if your right hand causes you to sin, cut it off and throw it away. For it is better that you lose one of your members than that your whole body go into hell.

To master spiritual energy, one must drive his or her energy upward from survival, pleasure, and power to love, creativity, insight, and spirituality. Sexual energy (second chakra) is the most powerful energy one can experience. That is why codependency in relationships is such an epidemic in our culture. As a society, must learn to refocus the energy arising from such overwhelming desire for sexual pleasure and aim it toward the service of God. When one learns to lust for God with the intensity one lust sexually for a man or woman, traversing the spiritual path becomes effortless.

In ancient times, "You shall not commit adultery" was the commandment. In modern times, the sadly degrading mantra "sex sells", has invaded our minds and the minds of our children with promiscuous images at every turn of the page or click of the mouse. Christ said, "If your right eye makes you stumble, tear it out… for it is better to lose one of the parts of your body than for your whole body to be thrown in hell." The single eye alluded to in this statement is a subtle reference to opening the third eye through the practice of meditation. When we learn to listen to our intuitional center, the need to be told what to do by everyone around us goes away. It becomes possible to truly live from the heart and listen to our intuition.

Another way of saying this is, "Where the mind goes, the body follows." We often look for love in all the wrong places. If you go to a bar looking to find a mate, it is doubtful you will find anything more than a one night stand. If you saturate your mind with pornography or even pictures of scantily dressed men or women, you become focus on the cheap, temporary, external nature of a person instead of the eternal infinite soul inside them. Forget about a playmate, focus on attracting and uniting with a soulmate. Instead of trying to *fall* in love, seek out relationships where you can *rise* in love. Find a partner who helps you elevate your innate levels of greatness. God will guide you in the right direction. All we must do is look and listen in the right places. This person will not likely look or act like you had originally imagined. The soulmate is not what our ego wants, rather it is what the soul needs for its development and maturation.

Divorce 5:31-32

It was also said, 'Whoever divorces his wife, let him give her a certificate of divorce.' But I say to you that everyone who divorces his wife, except on the ground of sexual immorality, makes her commit adultery, and whoever marries a divorced woman commits adultery.

It blows my mind to realize that 50 percent of all marriages in the United States end in divorce. This phenomenon is the result of placing greater value on lusting than loving. Unlike in the time of Christ, divorce is entirely acceptable in the modern age. Regardless of this fact, marriage is a sacred commitment not to be taken lightly. "Through the good times and the bad." There are ups and downs in every relationship. Be willing and humble enough to seek professional help if need be to make it through the hard times. When we get emotionally attached in relationships, it becomes difficult to utilize sound objective judgment. Therefore, it is so important to seek the guidance of a knowledgeable third party. It does not mean that you are weak or your relationship is failing. Quite the opposite, it means you love each other enough that you are willing to go to any lengths, putting the ego aside, to make the marriage work. Seeking help is an entirely honorable and admirably humble endeavor for married couples.

If you have made earnest effort and the marriage cannot be saved, you must surrender and let go of the attachment. When a relationship ceases to support both parties to advance in their spiritual evolution, it is no longer fulfilling its purpose. Every relationship is unique, and breakups are rarely ever easy. In this case loving the other person means letting them go. In granting them freedom, you grant yourself freedom. Do not judge or blame and you will not need to forgive. Accept the greater driving force behind all things, God. Meditation is an invaluable tool to keep your life in alignment when going through any difficult, life-changing situation.

Vows 5:33-37

Again, you have heard that it was said to those of old, 'You shall not swear falsely, but shall perform to the Lord what you have sworn.' But I say to you, do not take an oath at all, either by heaven, for it is the throne of God, or by the earth, for it is his footstool, or by Jerusalem, for it is the city of the great King. And do not take an oath by your head, for you cannot make one hair white or black. Let what you say be simply 'Yes' or 'No'; anything more than this comes from evil.

    It is unnecessary to swear to anything outside of yourself when accomplishing a task. To the spiritual aspirant, what is of utmost importance is to follow the heart. Learning to listen to our intuition and follow the guidance that flows from our inner self is an invaluable tool. Respecting others begins with the most basic skill of making and keeping agreements. If you cannot commit to an engagement, be honest. Say no in the beginning so all parties involved can continue with their purpose.

    On the other hand, when you do make a commitment with anyone, be it family, friends, work, in the spiritual/religious community, honor that commitment. Show up on time. Be physically and mentally prepared for the labor of love you agreed to participate in. In "The Prophet" Kahlil Gibran wrote, "When you work you are a flute through whose heart the whispering of the hours turns to music. Which of you would be a reed, dumb and silent, when all else sings in unison."

    When you work for the well-being of another, you are serving the divine in them, you are directly serving God. Keeping our agreements is an essential step to recognizing our piece in the whole, the innate interconnectedness of all life.

Revenge 5:38-41

You have heard that it was said, 'An eye for an eye and a tooth for a tooth.' But I say to you, do not resist the one who is evil. But if anyone slaps you on the right cheek, turn to him the other also. And if anyone would sue you and take your tunic, let him have your cloak as well. And if anyone forces you to go one mile, go with him two miles. Give to the one who begs from you, and do not refuse the one who would borrow from you.

When I was a young boy, I remember one day hearing a rabbi's sermon in a synagogue discussing a section in the book of Leviticus covering the topic of "an eye for an eye, a tooth for a tooth". Even at such a tender age, I knew there was something inherently wrong with this philosophy.

Yogi Ji once told me a story I call "The Spitting Buddha". One day Buddha was walking up the street with his disciple. A man came up to the Buddha and spit in his face. Buddha put his hands together in Namaste, bowed and said, "thank you" and then walked away.

The disciple was very troubled by what had just happened. He could not believe his teacher would allow this man to spit in his face and do nothing about it. The disciple even began to question whether he should be following Buddha in the first place.

The disciple asked his teacher why all he did was thank his aggressor. The Buddha smiled and said, "I've been waiting for that."

Karma is a tricky game. Someone does something nice to you; you do something nice back. Someone does something mean to you and you do something mean back. The world operates in a state of reaction. You don't win the game of karma by reacting. If karma were measured by points, positive points for good actions, negative points for bad actions, to be at zero points would be the goal. You win the game by not playing it. You break the cycle when you stop going around in circles, when you respond instead of react to a situation

In Western society, we are always focusing on rewards and consequences. This type of thinking keeps us trapped like a hamster on a wheel. We only act a certain way to achieve a desired reward.

To win the game of karma, you must learn make decisions because they are in alignment with your values, not because they will have a positive or negative outcome. This type of decision making will make the world a much more loving place. You must learn to respond instead of react. When you react, you act instinctively, in an animalistic way, countering a force, moving in a different direction, continuing to running on the hamster wheel of karma. When you respond, you choose the most righteous course of action possible, regardless of the results, because it is in alignment with your truth.

Buddha responded to being spit upon because he realized where he stood in the cycle of karma. Obviously, he had harmed someone in the past and this was his opportunity to right his wrongs, taking him back to zero in the game of karma. He could have spit back or hit the man, but this would have only continued the vicious cycle. That would have been a reaction.

In Sanskrit, there is a very beautiful word, "dharma". There is no direct English translation. In Japanese, there is a similar term, "bushido". This means the way of the warrior. It refers to the path a samurai had to take to live righteously and realize his purpose. Dharma is like this, the path of righteousness.

In our modern society for us to truly know our purpose in life, we must live righteously, instead of out of desire for the fruits of our labor. Yes, it is good to make money at the end of the day, but this should not be why we act in the first place. We act to be of service to others, because it is the right thing to do and in alignment with our hearts' journey. You will be blessed in the end. But receiving the blessing should not be the inspiration for action. Following your dharma, staying true to your course, finding your purpose in life is why you act. Bless those who curse you. There is no need to continue playing the game of karma.

Watching a movie about Krishna Das called "Fierce Grace", I heard another wonderful story about someone complimenting the kirtan wallah (a spiritual aspirant who chants devotionally as a meditation) Krishna Das on his jacket, "That is a lovely jacket". Krishna Das took off his jacket and gave it to the man. The man said, "I can't take this jacket, it's yours." Krishna Das replied, "There are many jackets in the world". Giving always feels much better than clinging or holding onto material items. In giving you are the one who is really receiving. We live in an abundant world. To tune into this abundance, you cannot hold back the current of giving energy. Like water, you must let this energy flow so it can come back to you tenfold. If rivers did not empty into the ocean, where would water come from to replenish the rivers? Operating out of an abundance mindset will only attract more abundance!

Giving is the embodiment of trust in the universe. It is the realization that God will, and always has, taken care of your needs, especially when you care for the well-being of others. The more you give, the more you get in return. This is true in all aspects of life. It could be in terms of money, work, material goods, even love itself. The sooner you begin to give unconditionally, the sooner you will begin to receive immeasurably.

Loving Your Enemies 5:43-48

You have heard that it was said, 'You shall love your neighbor and hate your enemy.' But I say to you, love your enemies and pray for those who persecute you, so that you may be sons of your Father who is in heaven. For he makes his sun rise on the evil and on the good, and sends rain on the just and on the unjust. For if you love those who love you, what reward do you have? Do not even the tax collectors do the same? And if you greet only your brothers, what more are you doing than others? Do not even the Gentiles do the same? You therefore must be perfect, as your heavenly Father is perfect.

It is all too easy to love those who love you. The saintly love their aggressors. We should all learn to love those challenging people in our lives. Without them, how could we ever grow, learn, overcome obstacles, or cultivate the ability to be compassionate?

I once heard a story about Meister Eckhart. He led a secluded spiritual community. One day, a very rude, disrespectful, lazy man showed up to the community. The new arrival quickly agitated all the community's members. He would not do his share of work and he maintained the worst of attitudes. A few months later, the new arrival suddenly up and left the community. Meister Eckhart quickly chased down the rude man, begged him to stay, even offered to pay him a salary if he stayed. Obviously, the man came back. The members of the community were furious when they found out what their teacher had done. They asked him, "Why?" He responded, "Without this man living here, how would you ever learn compassion."

Learn to see those who challenge you as a blessing. Those who hurt us, give us the opportunity to overcome the game of karma and develop a true practice of acceptance and compassion, to put love into action. Giving others a chance is giving yourself a chance to love. God loves everyone and everything under the sun. Everyone is on their own unique path and at a different place in their own spiritual evolution. By loving and honoring them, you love and honor God in the process.

Giving to the Needy 6:1-4

Beware of practicing your righteousness before other people in order to be seen by them, for then you will have no reward from your Father who is in heaven. Thus, when you give to the needy, sound no trumpet before you, as the hypocrites do in the synagogues and in the streets, that they may be praised by others. Truly, I say to you, they have received their reward. But when you give to the needy, do not let your left hand know what your right hand is doing, so that your giving may be in secret. And your Father who sees in secret will reward you.

Being self-righteous and universally righteous are two very different disciplines. The self-righteous serve only to better themselves. They serve the small self, the sense of "I", "me", or "mine". They work only for the satisfaction of the ego. The universally righteous understand the value in selfless service. They are altruistic and operate with great care and devotion for the well-being of others. Those who truly strive for righteousness through selfless service serve the Higher Self. They have ascended the ego having obtained employment for the divine.

Gandhi mastered the art of selfless service. I honor Gandhi by quoting him here, "One who would serve will not waste a thought on his own comforts, which he leaves to be attended to or neglected by his Master on High". The faith required to give selflessly demonstrates an unswerving realization and devotion to the divine. We help others not for recognition but because it is the right thing to do. There is a concept in Judaism that comes to mind called mitzvoth. It means duty. Our duty, our purpose on this planet is to serve the

Master on High through a dedication for the well-being of each other.

A sure-fire method to take the ego out of the equation when giving is to give anonymously. No one needs to know it was you. Only the ego needs recognition. If a family in your neighborhood is struggling to put food on the table, leave an anonymous, bountiful care package at their door. If a friend tells you of trouble in paying a specific bill, pay their bill for them without saying a word about it. Giving in such a manner shows God you are grateful for what He has given you. When people show you gratitude for your assistance, you want to give them more. We were created in His image and should embody our innate spiritual characteristics in all actions. By giving, you are proving to the universe you are ready to receive more.

Prayers and Fasting 6:5-18

And when you pray, you must not be like the hypocrites. For they love to stand and pray in the synagogues and at the street corners, that they may be seen by others. Truly, I say to you, they have received their reward. But when you pray, go into your room and shut the door and pray to your Father who is in secret. And your Father who sees in secret will reward you.

And when you pray, do not heap up empty phrases as the Gentiles do, for they think that they will be heard for their many words. Do not be like them, for your Father knows what you need before you ask him. Pray then like this:

"Our Father in heaven, hallowed be your name, Your kingdom come, your will be done, on earth as it is in heaven. Give us this day our daily bread, and forgive us our debts, as we also have forgiven our debtors. And lead us not into temptation, but deliver us from evil. For if you forgive others their trespasses, your heavenly Father will also forgive you, but if

you do not forgive others their trespasses, neither will your Father forgive your trespasses.

And when you fast, do not look gloomy like the hypocrites, for they disfigure their faces that their fasting may be seen by others. Truly, I say to you, they have received their reward. But when you fast, anoint your head and wash your face, that your fasting may not be seen by others but by your Father who is in secret. And your Father who sees in secret will reward you.

Prayer, meditation, and all other spiritual practices are not performed for external appearances rather to produce internal revelation. Fasting for physical reasons like losing weight increases attachment to the body. When undertaken for spiritual reasons, fasting heightens one's vibration in turn creating a sense of detachment from the body. To make any meaningful lasting effect in the outer world we must first transform our inner world.

Seek out a teacher, someone who can guide you in the ancient esoteric art of spiritual discipline. These practices are not to be taken lightly, instead to be performed reverently. Call out to God late in the night, as long as it takes, until your hearts yearning is answered. And trust me on this, He will answer the call, maybe not in the way you expect but you will receive guidance. Dedicate a space or room in your home to this practice. Honor your practice by adhering to it consistently at a specifically dedicated time every day.

Practice with consciousness to avoid your austerity from becoming mechanical. Practice with devotion prevents tediousness. With enough effort and consistency, results will manifest in your life. With a heroic effort and uninterrupted consistency, your life becomes your meditation. Each breach, every movement becomes a devotional offering to the God.

Mastering life itself through spiritual discipline is the realization of enlightenment. This is the highest blessing you can bestow upon yourself.

Fasting, going into silence, or any other denunciatory practice is performed for the betterment of the self and is done out of devotion. Do not make a show, fashion statement or any other ego trip out of the practice. These methods are not meant to impress anyone, rather to inspire the ultimate connection to the inner world. Shopping at a high-end yoga clothing store

does not make an enlightened yogi. Mala beads are not meant to be worn like a necklace or as a fashion accessory but to be used for meditation on the Highest. Divine union is the result of an immense amount of effort, the culmination of an incredible journey, an indescribable blessing of the creator. Instead of talking worldly talk, place all value in walking the spiritual walk.

Money and Possessions 6:19-34

Do not lay up for yourselves treasures on earth, where moth and rust destroy and where thieves break in and steal, but lay up for yourselves treasures in heaven, where neither moth nor rust destroys and where thieves do not break in and steal. For where your treasure is, there your heart will be also. The eye is the lamp of the body. So, if your eye is healthy, your whole body will be full of light, but if your eye is bad, your whole body will be full of darkness. If then the light in you is darkness, how great is the darkness! No one can serve two masters, for either he will hate the one and love the other, or he will be devoted to the one and despise the other. You cannot serve God and money.

Therefore, I tell you, do not be anxious about your life, what you will eat or what you will drink, nor about your body, what you will put on. Is not life more than food, and the body more than clothing? Look at the birds of the air: they neither sow

nor reap nor gather into barns, and yet your heavenly Father feeds them. Are you not of more value than they? And which of you by being anxious can add a single hour to his span of life? And why are you anxious about clothing? Consider the lilies of the field, how they grow: they neither toil nor spin, yet I tell you, even Solomon in all his glory was not arrayed like one of these. [30] But if God so clothes the grass of the field, which today is alive and tomorrow is thrown into the oven, will he not much more clothe you, O you of little faith? Therefore, do not be anxious, saying, 'What shall we eat?' or 'What shall we drink?' or 'What shall we wear?' For the Gentiles seek after all these things, and your heavenly Father knows that you need them all. But seek first the kingdom of God and his righteousness, and all these things will be added to you.

Therefore, do not be anxious about tomorrow, for tomorrow will be anxious for itself. Sufficient for the day is its own trouble.

Modesty is the key to material freedom. Always place precedence on spirituality before materialism. Short-term gratification equals long term pain. When we defer gratification, not only the potential but the reality of long-term happiness opens to you. Focusing on and valuing the permanent over the impermanent is the way to create outer peace by way of the inner world. Even the words printed on this very page are subject to destruction via the passage of time. The wisdom that permeates from the inner world is timeless and will remain forever true.

You cannot serve both the spiritual and the material world at the same time. There can only be one master. Since everyone must derive guidance from one source or another, choose to seek guidance from the highest source. Leave what belongs to the world to the world and give what is eternal to

Thou. When we place credence on connecting to an inner heaven, the outer world quickly aligns with the inner vision.

Create a clarity within all levels of self from the physical body, breath body, emotional body, intellectual body, and the spiritual body. When we learn to polish each lens of the self, the inner light becomes magnified by the luminosity of the entire authentic self. Thus, the inner light becomes apparently radiant to the outer world.

When you live your purpose, the universe will move mountains to assist you in manifesting your greatness. The members of the animal kingdom do not waste energy worrying whether they will have enough to last until tomorrow. They live knowing the Provider will look after their every need. If God takes care of the plant and animal kingdom in such a way, why would He not look after our well-being in the same manner? The world is analogous to the body of God, we humans are the right hand. The life force of the body, the blood flows equally throughout each crevasse of the whole. Trusting in the omnipotence of the whole system puts one's heart at peace.

There is never any reason to worry. There is absolutely no benefit to be derived from worrying. The greatest benefit can be discovered by living in peace and harmony. In that which you cannot control, there is no need to worry because you cannot control it. That which you can control, you can control so there is no need to worry about it. Understanding this viewpoint eradicates the illusion of any benefit to worrying.

Do Not Judge Others 7:1-6

Judge not, that you be not judged. For with the judgment you pronounce you will be judged, and with the measure you use it will be measured to you. Why do you see the speck that is in your brother's eye, but do not notice the log that is in your own eye? Or how can you say to your brother, 'Let me take

the speck out of your eye,' when there is the log in your own eye? You hypocrite, first take the log out of your own eye, and then you will see clearly to take the speck out of your brother's eye. Do not give dogs what is holy, and do not throw your pearls before pigs, lest they trample them underfoot and turn to attack you.

Wayne Dyer said, "There is no need to forgive because there is no need to blame or judge others." Passing judgment is yet another feeble attempt of the ego to draw lines of separation dividing the unity of the whole. Others are a mirror for us to see ourselves. When we judge others, it is because we are unhappy with some aspect of ourselves we recognize in their words or actions. When we judge others, we judge ourselves. Pointing out the imperfections of others is a vain attempt to shift the light away from our own shortcomings and stall the inevitable evolution of the soul.

Practicing acceptance, being apathetic, and living compassionately are the alternatives to blaming others for our interpretations of their actions. It is not our duty to blame or judge others. It is the duty of the spiritual aspirant to cultivate love toward all things under the divine umbrella regardless of any temporary circumstance.

A notorious trademark of the ego is identification with thought. When we lose sight of our real self and become conditioned to be enslaved by the mind, the ego begins to pass judgment and cast blame. *The ego requires forgiveness.* Giving up control of our minds, passing over the reins of the vehicle of our actions to the unconscious thought process surrenders all possibility of conscious discernment. The real self operates from the seat of the heart. The real self only knows love. This most essential layer of the self prefers to give a hug instead of point the finger. Judgment divides the planet; love unites the world. When you operate in love, you cease to point out others misgivings and act as the catalyst for the transformation of all. Embodying these teaching will change the world.

In the second part of this teaching, Christ reminds us that we must maintain an uplifting inner circle of friends we trust. Do not share the pearls of wisdom discovered on your spiritual journey with those who are not on a similar path to your own. Their doubts and insecurities will create an apathy of faith, belief, and understanding needed to follow your own path.

Do not try to wake those who are still sleeping to the truth of the spiritual dimension lest they be angry with you. They will wake up and see the light when are ready. Surround yourself with those like-souled individuals who will assist you in heightening your vibrations.

Effective Prayer 7:7-11

Ask, and it will be given to you; seek, and you will find; knock, and it will be opened to you. For everyone who asks receives, and the one who seeks finds, and to the one who knocks it will be opened. Or which one of you, if his son asks him for bread, will give him a stone? Or if he asks for a fish, will give him a serpent? If you then, who are evil, know how to give good gifts to your children, how much more will your Father who is in heaven give good things to those who ask him!

The self-actualized are growth motivated. This means they realize they already have all they will ever need within themselves. The practice of prayer is a method of physical manifestation. Self-love is being honest enough with ourselves to admit what we need instead of what we want (are you starting to see a pattern with love?). In this manner, we can ask the universal essence to manifest our needs. Love is not this gushy, comfortable, easy thing, but it is empowering. Love is the energy that powers the entire universe. So automatically, when we ask for what we really need, it could be for survival, growth, spiritual connection or anything else, the need is fulfilled in front of our very eyes. Almost like magic. Love is so powerful that it often appears magical. As a parent loves a child so much they will provide their child with anything he or she needs to grow and learn, so too does the Universal Parent enrich our lives with what we need to grow and learn. Real prayer is not asking for the satisfaction of material desires. Real prayer is an inquiry into how to best serve the divine will. It is asking for the strength to accomplish our purpose even if we do not yet clearly recognize that purpose. Revel in gratitude for the abundant love that enriches every inch of the universe at each moment.

The Golden Rule 7:12-14

So, whatever you wish that others would do to you, do also to them, for this is the Law and the Prophets. Enter by the narrow gate. For the gate is wide and the way is easy that leads to destruction, and those who enter by it are many. For the gate is narrow and the way is hard that leads to life, and those who find it are few.

Isaac Newton's third law of gravity is in perfect alignment with the golden rule, "Every action has an equal and opposite reaction". When you "treat people the same way you want them to treat you" as the golden rule says, you are recognizing reciprocity behind all thoughts, words, and actions. Einstein taught that energy could neither be created nor destroyed only transformed from one state to another. That which we think, say, and do was inspired either by something in or outside of ourselves. The individual has the power to transform that energy in whichever way he or she sees fit. The way we interpret and process this energy determines the quality of energy we will receive in return. When a person chooses to manifest hate, anger, greed, or express other traits of discontent in the world, they are responsible for the shadow they cast. When that person instead chooses to be grateful, compassionate, sympathetic, or exhibit any other trait of love, they consciously decide to shine that light in the world. The golden rule is a simple yet extremely important universal law that teaches us how to harvest the best result in all aspect of life.

The second section of this portion describes the highest path in life is taken by entering the city through the narrow instead of a wide gate. In another portion of the Bible, Jesus describes entering heaven as difficult as passing through the eye of a needle. In Aramaic, the word used to describe a narrow city gate is the same word for the eye of a needle. In Christ's double entendre, we are taught that to enter heaven, we must step off our high horse and humbly walk into the city of heaven. Humility is the highest and most righteous path to be taken. The ego is the cause of all suffering while paradoxically, allowing oneself to experience suffering is what dissolves the ego. Looking beyond the mechanism of the mind, we see we are not the ego or our thoughts, instead our true self is that which is thinking. From our essence, we can recognize humility and self-esteem is the same thing! This statement holds much gravity. By realizing that all life is united, we are humbled by accepting our part in the whole. At the same time, we are empowered by serving a higher purpose. The blissful path of spirit can only be taken in humility.

The Tree and Its Fruit 7:15-20

Beware of false prophets, who come to you in sheep's clothing but inwardly are ravenous wolves. You will recognize them by their fruits. Are grapes gathered from thorn bushes, or figs from thistles? So, every healthy tree bears good fruit, but the diseased tree bears bad fruit. A healthy tree cannot bear bad fruit, nor can a diseased tree bear good fruit. Every tree that does not bear good fruit is cut down and thrown into the fire. Thus, you will recognize them by their fruits.

Every student needs a teacher. God is the greatest Guru. Usually an intermediary is required, at least in the beginning, to strengthen and clarify the signal. It is often said,

"When the student is ready the teacher appears". Following your intuition guides you in the direction of your purpose. You will come across many different teachers on your journey. Opportunities to learn manifest in a multitude of forms. Emotional experiences, overcoming an injury, dealing with a challenging person are all examples of potential learning opportunities. Every quote used in this book represents a specific lesson I have learned from different teachers through their work. Those who are guided to personally meet a living spiritual master in this lifetime are truly blessed. A spiritual aspirant requires a teacher's guidance to find the right direction. Attempting to traverse the spiritual path without a teacher is like aiming for the bull's-eye while wearing a blindfold.

Usually the reluctant master proves to be more capable than the eager one. The former acknowledges the great responsibility of guiding another. He or she will not take the responsibility lightly, yet will demands much. The capable guide teaches by giving you obstacles and challenges to overcome. It is not an easy path by any means. The eager teacher is all too often an egotistical one. Choose a teacher who you trust and who has produced tangible results. There should be other students of the teacher who have attained the results you desire. Be discerning, but when you make the commitment, devote yourself whole-heartedly and dedicate all effort to attaining the goal. Avoid the desire to switch teachers when the lessons are difficult.

Like digging a well in search of water, if you give up before striking water and begin digging another hole, you will never find water wasting much energy in the process. Dig one hole. Trust one teacher and continue the search until quenching the spiritual thirst. Sometimes it will appear not much progress is being made. Often when digging a well, you hit a particularly dense patch of dirt. This section is only temporary and does not negate the work you have done to get to that point. Keep working and you will get through the tough times and become all the stronger for it.

True Disciples 7:21-23

Not everyone who says to me, 'Lord, Lord,' will enter the kingdom of heaven, but the one who does the will of my Father who is in heaven. On that day many will say to me, 'Lord, Lord, did we not prophesy in your name, and cast out demons in your name, and do many mighty works in your name?' And then will I declare to them, 'I never knew you; depart from me, you workers of lawlessness.'

Crying out the name of God will not get you into heaven. Chanting the sacred mantra alone will not make you enlightened. When your life embodies the divine, when your life becomes the living word, you create heaven in the world. Going through the motions, mechanically performing a spiritual discipline accomplishes little or nothing. By enhancing the ability to be aware, consistently being awake in each moment, we allow Presence to permeate every layer of being. It is not enough to devote one's actions to God. Instead, seek to accurately follow the divine will, the aspirant honors the Highest energy in the universe.

Consistent spiritual practice is important but performing an austerity is only half the battle. When meditation becomes a way of living instead of a temporary performance, you have achieved the goal. Taking spirituality outside of the religious context by becoming a living manifestation of the word allows one to see every place as holy. Staying conscious of the Source within at each moment allows one to see every person, place, and thing as sacred. I once hear Eckhart Tolle say he did not separate a time for spiritual practice. His presence in every moment made his very life itself the practice. Instead of honoring certain occurrences as miracles, dedicate life itself as a miracle by living in accordance with the universal will. It is entirely possible to live in this body of flesh but see through the eyes of God.

Building a Solid Foundation 7:24-29

Everyone then who hears these words of mine and does them will be like a wise man who built his house on the rock. And the rain fell, and the floods came, and the winds blew and beat on that house, but it did not fall, because it had been founded on the rock. And everyone who hears these words of mine and does not do them will be like a foolish man who built his house on the sand. And the rain fell, and the floods came, and the winds blew and beat against that house, and it fell, and great was the fall of it. And when Jesus finished these sayings, the crowds were astonished at his teaching, [29] for he was teaching them as one who had authority, and not as their scribes.

The teachings of Jesus covered in the Sermon on the Mount are powerful and should be incorporated into every aspect of life. "Everyone who hears these words and acts on them may be compared to a wise man who builds his house on the rock". The house stands through all turbulent storms because it is grounded on a steady foundation. Allow the teachings from all ancient sources of wisdom to act as your foundation. Take the time to assimilate these truths into your life and you will remain unmoved through the turbulent experiences in life.

Slow growth is much safer than fast, uncontrolled growth. A tree that has roots grown deep over many years stands through the most intense storms. A tree that sprouts up quickly but does not dedicate energy to growing its root system falls over in the first wind. Allow the truth of these ancient wisdom teachings to be your roots, study them constantly. Meditation is the trunk of the tree connecting the physical and the spiritual selves. The branches, leaves, and fruit of the tree are the flowering of your life in the world. In this method, the spiritual aspirant remains grounded and unmoved by squalls of the material world.

As the seekers of His time were amazed by the teachings of Christ, 2,000 years later, I am astonished by the simplicity, clarity, and relevance in the message. Incorporating these truths into my life has been a blessing. I encourage you to integrate these principles in your life as you walk the spiritual path.

Chapter 17: Illuminating the World

Degrees of Enlightenment

Heightened awareness or awakened consciousness can be divided into three categories: belief, knowing, and realization. I will define each category in this section.

Belief:

The Buddha taught all life is suffering. The first degree of enlightenment is the belief that suffering is the vehicle for personal evolution. Take a moment to ponder what led you to begin your spiritual journey. I can guarantee that everything was not wonderful in your life or going exactly as you planned at that moment. For me, the few years prior to beginning my spiritual journey were filled with all sorts of suffering such as substance abuse, legal problems, intense anger, fear, and shame just to name a few. Your reasons may not be as dramatic as mine or they may be even worse. The point I am getting at is this great suffering is the source of discontent which inspires the spiritual aspirant into action.

Suffering is God's call to journey inward into the wilderness of the subconscious through meditation. If everything in the world were peachy keen, everyone had more than enough money, and there were no difficulties or struggles, who would need God? Experiencing suffering is the blessing of hearing the celestial song. Obstacles are opportunities for divine communion. Instead of maintaining negative emotions about suffering, be grateful for the experiences which enable and encourage your progression. The belief in this universal truth is the first step to awakened consciousness.

Instead of questioning "why me?", in the face of such insurmountable difficulties, appreciate and understand the fact that you are being guided toward your own inevitable maturation. Instead of fighting the transformation, surrender and embrace your destiny. Coming to a place where you truly believe this reality is the first major junction on the journey toward your destiny.

When we accept our struggles and stride forward, empowerment springs forth from our soul and we become capable of greatness never imagined. We begin to work with the universe instead of against it. Embrace suffering, as it is the means to uncovering your true potential.

Knowing:

The second degree of enlightenment is a knowing that you are experiencing your current life circumstances for a reason. Whether you understand the significance of your current situation or not, you are established in the understanding there is a greater power operating at this moment and every moment of your life. You have stopped fighting what you like or dislike and embrace the current that has always been guiding you toward your highest potential. The self-pitying stage of your development has longed ceased to plague your mind. You embrace life's challenges with the knowing you are traversing the path of your destiny.

This paradigm shift gives you the ability to appreciate the things you have gained from difficult experiences. Maybe you were incarcerated and know that the experience gifted you with an indomitable will. Perhaps overcoming an addiction gave you the confidence and clarity you needed to manifest your destiny. Or possibly the painful ending of a romantic relationship allows you to experience the most important relationship, to fall in love with yourself. That is not to mention, the only way you can find the right partner is to leave the wrong partner. However difficult your situation may be, you know there is a means to an end, there is a reason you are going through your specific process.

In this stage of our consciousness, we know we are living our current life experiences for a reason and we choose to embrace it. It is so beautiful to allow oneself to experience the moment without aversion to pain or attachment to pleasure. All experiences in the physical reality are temporary and designed to guide us toward higher states of consciousness. Embrace each moment knowing there is a deeper meaning behind each superficial experience. Regardless whether an event is traditionally labeled with a designation of good or bad, a profound, subtle spiritual lesson awaits to be uncovered by allowing yourself to experience that event with your presence. Recognize the reason for having to experience unpleasant moments or setbacks in life is to unlock the wisdom of a deep seeded truth that behind each obstacle awaits an opportunity. Humility is the key to this lock. Acceptance is the ability to turn the key and coalesce each lesson and evolve.

Realization:

The highest degree of consciousness is a subtle shift from the knowing we experience each circumstance for a reason, but it makes all the difference in the world. This is the realization of our purpose in life. Realize everything that has ever happened, is currently happening, or will happen in your life is not by accident, but by design. Call it whatever you like, but there is a power guiding you from your first breath to your last to realize a specific purpose in creation.

Recall a struggle you experienced one year ago, how has that struggle guided you toward realizing the life's path you are on right now? Think back 10 years or even as far back as you can remember in your childhood. Every experience in life has led you to exactly where you are right now in this very moment.

The sooner you realize your reason for being, the sooner you can direct all your energy on target toward achieving your purpose.

Everyone came into existence for a specific purpose. The soul has always and will always exist. I came from the infinite and will return in a universal blink of an eye. Our existence in our current form of the human body is only a momentary experience in the eternal life of the soul. All that being said, the soul would only take its current form for a specific reason, to accomplish a purpose. This is your purpose in life. Each tradition has a different term describing purpose, such as dharma, bushido, Tao, and mitzvoth. As you realize your destined way in life, all the infinite power will start moving mountains to help you achieve your purpose. The impossible becomes easy. Your material desires fade away yet actualize at the same time. It is beyond a matter of success because you are realizing your purpose. The satisfaction of a job well done, a life well lived is payment enough yet you are compensated in every way possible.

I am ecstatic for you to take this step in your journey. Your dreams are already coming true as you realize you are on purpose in your life. Do not waste a single sacred moment. Infinite love flows through you, let yourself swim and play in its current.

Living with awareness of the levels of Enlightenment is not easy but this practice will help you end the cycle of suffering and live in greater harmony with the divine will. When you are going through a moment of crisis (and remember crisis can only last for a temporary moment), take yourself through each level of enlightenment. Ask yourself how maintaining the belief that suffering is the catalyst for evolution is driving you further down the course of your personal development? Next probe your mind for the hidden reason in the circumstance you are currently overcoming. Finally admit to yourself that this obstacle is guiding you toward realizing your purpose in life.

Completing this practice requires unprecedented levels of self-honesty. Only by thinking correctly and maintaining a reality based mind state will you be able to recognize and advance your current state of illumination. Take a moment and think of the three best things that have ever happened to you in your life. Now think of the three worst things that have ever happened to you in your life. Finally, consider how these six occurrences are integrated and entirely dependent on each other. None of the good things in our lives could happen without the bad.

I can share my experience of this exercise with you as an example. This first extraordinary thing I can think of that has happened to me in life was to born as the only child of two amazing open-minded, spiritual parents who could provide for my every physical need while encouraging me to determine my own life's course. They did this without judgment or overly exerting their personal desires on me. The second best think I can think of that took place my life was my second birth into the spiritual life. I discovered this path through yoga and meditation. The third biggest accomplishment in my life has been the completion of this book.

The three worst things that have happened to me are less comfortable to admit and discuss. The first is the ending of my past life. No one dies by enjoyable or comfortable circumstances. The second was living in a boarding school in Mexico from the age of 16 to 18 where I was physically and emotionally abused. It was an extremely painful and traumatic time in my life. The third was spending 15 months in jail where I experienced widespread violence, racism, and hatred.

It is quite remarkable how each of these events is relate. If I did not die in my past life, how could I be born into my new life? After death, the soul goes back to its divine essence and to again manifest in the physical world the soul must temporarily depart the celestial realm. Had my previous life experience not ended, my current experience could never have begun.

Going to that horrible school in Mexico and living in such deplorable conditions led me to feel so angry all I wanted to do was fight. I decided to get in to mixed martial arts and found studying jiu-jitsu to be my path. I learned the best Brazilian jiu-jitsu practitioners practiced yoga to increase flexibility, strength and proprioception. Summing it all up, going to the boarding school led me to such levels of anger all I wanted to was fight. Fighting led me to yoga, which was the beginning of my spiritual awakening.

Spending time in jail gave me the opportunity to deepen my spiritual study and create such consistency in my yoga and meditation practice that I could cultivate the clarity required to produce the work you are now reading! It is amazing, empowering, and uplifting for me to reminisce on my life challenges and recognize how they were the fulcrums for my greatest achievements. Only by being rigorously and introspectively honest with myself could I ever realize these connections.

During my first two challenges, I did not recognize any of these levels of enlightenment, as I was not yet spiritually awake. As my struggles in jail were occurring I recognized how my suffering drove me deeper into an experience of reality that was unknown to me before. I knew and was cognizant there was a reason I had to go through the experience. Toward the end of my time in jail, I realized by conveying the lessons I learned, I could positively impact the world by sharing the wisdom gained from writing this book. I had begun to live my purpose.

Challenges will always present themselves. We will continuously be given the opportunity to learn and grow by overcoming our struggles. The key is to recognize the purpose in each struggle as it is taking place. This state of realization alleviates most if not all suffering allowing one to operate from a place of gratitude and understanding. We can choose to be dragged by God toward our purpose or walk with Him hand-inhand. The individual choice exists to suffer or to thrive in life; to live in heaven or hell. The level of appreciation is like a thermostat. By being grateful, we choose to lower the temperature cooling the heavenly air encompassing all things. Ingratitude raises the temperature to uncomfortable levels of suffering and discontent. You choose how you use your spiritual power.

Global Enlightenment

Since we are all one organism on this planet, can any of us really be enlightened without all of us being illuminated?

The body is made up of individual cells. When you look at the homeostasis of a single cell, it can be in one of two states, either living or dying. The light switch is either on or off. And it is so with us as individual beings. The light in us is either on or off. It cannot be just a little bit on. There is no dimmer switch. We are either immersed in the darkness of ignorance or overflowing in the abundant light of awareness. There is no in between. Individual beings are like cells of the planet. Collectively we determine whether we live in a world radiating light or are lost in darkness.

To become an enlightened yogi, living in a cave is admirable undertaking. Such a being would heighten the collective energy from that space to a certain degree, but that is the easy path. To turn away and hide from the world, anybody could reach heightened states of consciousness. Alternatively, by learning to deal with difficult people, you heighten your consciousness. Difficult people facilitate the learning and growth processes. Your impact on the planet will be much greater learning to raise your awareness where it is needed most, right here in society.

The planet is in a state of crisis. Most the individual cells (people) are in a state of decline, de-evolution, one of constant darkness. What we need is not to build another dam to control the flow of energy, but instead to change the direction of the flow of the river. Instead of allowing our internal energy to plummet, individuals must learn to direct that energy toward the spiritual realm. Collectively society must learn to balance each energy center allowing spiritual power to ceaselessly flow through each being.

You can read of this global crisis in the newspapers daily. The annual sea level is rising, by an amount that can be measured in feet. This may not seem much to those whose focus does not extend much past the weekend. When people realize at this rate by the end of their children's lifetimes all the major seaside cities on the planet will no longer exist, a sense of urgency will hopefully begin to develop.

We are so conditioned in our society by consumerism and materialism we have lost our bearings. When the Indians saw Europeans fighting to control more than an individual could ever use, they recognized such behavior as a symptom of mental imbalance. Native American culture defined success as being able to live in harmony with the land. Disharmony with the land is an illness, a form of insanity The Native Americans believed to be successful one must have provided for the next seven generations in their lifetime. This did not mean to horde enough food, land, or money to provide for their descendants, but for the impressions of their values to leave a lasting imprint of unity with the planet.

If we are all truly one organism, the highest level of enlightenment can only be obtained when we all reach this state of pure awareness, when we all achieve unity with each other and the planet. The time for awakening is now. We cannot afford to wait any longer. All the work of all the mystics, prophets, yogis, seers, divine incarnations all culminate to this moment right now inside you. This is the moment of your awakening. The moment for you to realize your unity with the divine. This is your initiation into the global community of enlightenment. Welcome and congratulations! The light in you is shining brightly and permeates through all levels of your self.

The enlightened mind is that which is firmly established in the art of seeking. Always look to deepen your spiritual connection. Constantly ask yourself, "How can I be of greater service?", and "How can I take this meditation of my life to the next level?" Keep searching as you go deeper each day toward your source.

It is now time for us to drop the barriers between cities, states, and countries and see this planet as one single organism, one global village. We all have a crucial role to play in this divine unification of the cosmos. Your personal task may be to teach others of the way, to create an eco-village, to lobby the government, or some other critical role in our planetary transformation. We all have an important part to play. There are an infinite number of tasks that must be undertaken. Only together can we accomplish this tremendous feat and save the world. Only you can define your specific purpose. Follow your heart in seeking divine guidance to discern your specific task. It is a crucial one. Change cannot take place without you.

The one thing that is certain is there is no time to waste. Our global conundrum is becoming dire. In every decision made, we must consider the benefit of the planet for at least the next seven generations. Now you may be thinking, this guy has gone off his rocker and wants us all to up and move to eco-villages. May you all and the planet be so blessed. Ask yourself, are you truly happy in this life of conditioned existence? Are you happy being told what to wear and what to eat by the consumer media? Are you happy slaving away at work every day to afford the lifestyle you are being told to live? Meditate on what happiness is and you will come to the realization that happiness is found within by living in harmony with the divine. As a society, we are out of harmony. As your consciousness is an individual cell to the cosmos, you can turn the light back on by realizing such harmony and following the guidance of your heart. The understanding to facilitate this transformation lies within you. Cultivate the courage. Live in the driver's seat of your heart, use enthusiasm as your fuel, and allow love to be your roadmap. Enlightenment is the destination but oh the journey. Your journey is made synchronously with the divine.

It is time for us to come together in love and in God and save the planet. All of Christ's teachings were for a purpose. All Buddha's teachings, all Krishna's teachings, along with all other ancient and modern mystics alike all culminate to this moment right now in your heart.

To become enlightened, you need one very important piece of spiritual technology, a mirror. Look in the mirror and see yourself as you really are, your true self, past every layer of conditioning. You will realize you are enlightened and always have been. Every single cell that creates your being is made entirely of light.

Traditionally, when a yogi took on a disciple, nothing was asked in payment until the student had attained the goal of enlightenment. Now it is time for me to ask for payment. What I ask of you now in return for sharing all these sacred esoteric teachings is that you give it all back to the world. Share what you have learned with everyone you can. Teach the principles and truths you have learned to all you come across. You can only keep what you have by giving it away. We all can only become enlightened to the highest degree when we scale that peak collectively. We live as one planet and have one heartbeat. Now that you know the truth, it is time to do something about it.

Blessings...

Bibliography

Aurobindo, S. (1995). *Looking from Within.* Twin Lakes, WI: Lotus Press.

Bachman, N. (2011). *The Path of the Yoga Sutras.* Boulder, CO: Sounds True.

Beckwith, M. B. (2008). *Spiritual Liberation.* Hillsboro, Or: Beyond Words.

Dyer, W. (1992). *Real Magic: Creating Miracles in Everday Life.* New York, NY: HaperCollins Publishing.

Dyer, W. (1998). *Wisdom of the Ages.* New York, NY: HaperCollins Publishing.

Dyer, W. (2001). *There's A Spiritual Solution To Every Problem.* New York, NY: HarperCollins Publishing.

Dyer, W. W. (2008). *Living the Wisdom of the Tao.* Hay House.

Easwaran, E. (1972). *Gandhi the Man.* Tomales, CA: Nilgiri Press.

Easwaran, E. (1985). *The Dhammapada.* Tomales, CA: Nilgiri Press.

Easwaran, E. (1987). *The Upanishads.* Tomales, CA: Nilgiri Press.

Easwaran, E. (2009). *The Mantram Hankbook.* Tomales, CA, Canada: Niligiri Press.

Easwaran, E. (2011). *Essence of the Bhagavad Gita.* Tomales, CA: Niligiri Press.

Fitzgerald, S. A. (2011). *The Original Gospel of Ramakrishna.* Bloomington, Indiana: World Wisdom.

Freeman, R. (2012). *The Mirror of Yoga: Awakening of the Intelligence of Body and Mind.* Boston, MA: Shambala.

Isherwood, C. (1965). *Ramakrishna and His Disciples.* Hollywood, California: Vedanta Press.

Isherwood, C. (2007). *How to Know God.* Hollywood, California: Vedanta Press.

King Jr., M. L. (1963). *Strength to Love.* Fortress Press, MN: Minneapolis.

Maharshi, R. (1972). *The Spiritual Teaching of Ramana Maharshi.* Boston, MA: Shambhala.

Menon, R. (2001). *The Ramayana.* New York: North Point Press.

Naimy, M. (2002). *The Book of Mirdad.* London, England: Watkins.

Osho. (1999). *Courage The Joy of Living Dangerously.* New York, NY: St. Martin's Griffin.

Pond, D. (1999). *Chakras For Beginners.* Woodbury, MN: Llewellyn Publications.

Rick Hanson, R. M. (2009). *Buddha's Brain: The Practical Neuroscience of Happiness, Love, and Wisdom.* Oakland, CA: New Harbinger Publications.

Tolle, E. (2005). *A New Earth Awakening to your Life's Purpose.* New York, NY: Penguin Group.